D1475972

GILBERT AND SULLIVAN

GILBERT & SULLIVAN
A Composite Photograph

GILBERT & SULLIVAN

A CRITICAL APPRECIATION OF
THE *SAVOY OPERAS* BY
A. H. GODWIN

With an introduction by
G. K. CHESTERTON

KENNIKAT PRESS, INC./PORT WASHINGTON, N. Y.

GILBERT & SULLIVAN

First published 1926
Reissued 1969 by Kennikat Press

Library of Congress Catalog Card No: 68-26216
Manufactured in the United States of America

INTRODUCTION

The best work of the Victorian age, perhaps the most Victorian work of the Victorian age, was its satire upon itself. It would be well if this were remembered more often by those who talk of nothing but its pomposity and conventionality. There was, indeed, a strain in it not only of pomposity but of hypocrisy; but like everything English, it was rather subtle. In so far as it existed it should be called rather humbug than hypocrisy, for hypocrisy implies intellectual clarity, and humbug suggests rather that convenient possession, a confused mind. The exclamation that a thing is all damned humbug is of the same sort as the exclamation that it is all damned nonsense. English humbug has had at least the comforting quality of nonsense, and something of that quality belongs even to the nonsense which made fun of the nonsense. And it will be found, I think, in the long run that this Victorian nonsense will prove more valuable than all that was considered the solid Victorian sense.

It is idle to prophesy about tastes and fashion; but to speak of the failure of the practical compromise of our great unwritten Constitution, for instance, is not to prophesy. It is merely to record. All that side of the British pomposity of the time has obviously collapsed in our time. The political balance and repose of the Victorians, the serious satisfaction of their social arrangements, is already a thing of the past; and perhaps this unbalanced absurdity may prove far more permanent in the future. But it is not only true of practical politics, which have become so exceedingly unpractical. It is true even of pure literature, which in one sense can always remain ideal. The Gilbert and Sullivan Operas can still be revived, and revived with complete popular success. I think it very doubtful whether " The Idylls of the King," if they were published now, would produce the same sort of effect as when they were published then. I doubt whether Longfellow would immediately obtain his large crowd or Browning his small one. It is not a question of the merits of the poetry or even of the truth of the criticism. People who talk thus about the appeal to posterity often seem to forget that posterity may be wrong—especially about the books that it has not read. Browning's work will always be worthy of study, just as Donne's work will always be worthy of study, but it would be rash to infer that it is always studied. Tennyson will always present certain triumphs of diction for those who are acquainted with the English language. But when Anglo-Saxon is talked all over the world, those acquainted with the English language may be comparatively few. There may be a very general neglect of the Victorian achievements, and as this will be merely an effect of time, it may be merely temporary. But as things stand, the Victorian monument which best supports and survives the change of fashion, is not the Laureate ode and office any more than the Albert Memorial: it is all that remains of the Savoy Opera.

But anyone who understands what was really to be said for and against the Victorian interlude or compromise will note with interest that the Victorian satirist did lash the age, in the old phrase ; and if in a sense he lashed lightly he also lashed with precision ; he touched the spot. He was an inquisitor, as waggish as his own Inquisitor in " The Gondoliers," but he did really persecute the rather hazy heresies of the hour. He did really persecute in the exact sense of pursue ; he tracked an untrue or unreasonable idea back to its first principle. Gilbert's gayest songs and most farcical rhymes are full of examples which a philosopher or a logician will value as real ideas or criticisms of ideas. And it was always the criticism really demanded by the half-formed ideas of the Victorians, those half-warmed fish which the Spooners of the age had in their hearts, but not very clearly in their heads. Any number of examples of this sort of thing could be given. For instance, nothing was more subtly false in the Victorians' conception of success than a certain conception of the elect who were above temptation.

x

There was a queer sort of cheery Calvinism in it ; a sort of jovial predestination. Certain social types, the good sportsman, the English lady, the frank and fearless English school boy (provided, of course, he were a public school boy), were regarded, not as heroes who had overcome the baser passions, but as gods who could never have been touched by them. The phraseology of the time testified to the notion again and again. Such people were not innocent of a crime ; they were " incapable " of it. Political corruption (which was increasing by leaps and bounds) was calmly ignored on the assumption of it being simply " impossible " in what was generally described as " a man of that position." Men who really preserved their honour under trials had no reward or recognition of their real merit, if they were of the sort in whom such things were supposed to be inconceivable. Everyone who has read the novels and newspapers of that time will recognise this formless impression, but not everybody could have put it into logical form. Yet it is pricked or stabbed with deadly precision in five or six absurd lines of a light refrain in " The Mikado " :

> " *We know him well,*
> *He cannot tell*
> *Untrue or groundless tales—*
> *He always tries*
> *To utter lies*
> *And every time he fails.*"

It is the same with the heresy that haunted the great Victorian virtue of patriotism. What was the matter with it was that it was a sort of unconscious shuffling of an unselfish into a selfish emotion. It was not so much that a man was proud of England, as that he was proud of being an Englishman, which is quite a different thing. Being proud of your country is only like being proud of your father or your friend ; it is not, in the spiritual and evil sense, really pride at all. But being proud of yourself for being a citizen of that country is really using something else as an excuse for being proud of yourself. Now, the logical or illogical point of that process is in the

*matter of merit, and the satirist really hits it with
the exactitude of a subtle theologian. It is a
question of how much there is implied some moral
superiority such as ought to be founded on the
individual will, and it could not be better exposed
than in the few words of that old familiar and
even rowdy song :*

> " *But in spite of all temptations
> To belong to other nations
> He remains an Englishman.*"

*The rapier of Voltaire could not have run a thing
more straight through the heart. Now the work
of Gilbert, especially in his operas, but very
notably also in his Bab Ballads, is full of triumphs
of that intellectual and even theoretical sort.
There was even something about him personally
not altogether unlike the tone of the theologian
and inquisitor ; his wit was staccato and sometimes harsh, and he was not happy in his own age
and atmosphere. It did not provide him with any
positive philosophy for which to fight, but that
was not his fault. He did fight for what he*

conceived to be common sense, and he found plenty of things that wanted fighting.

And then the odd thing happened that was like a lucky coincidence in a farce or a magic gift in a fairy tale. As it stood, his satire was really much too intelligent to be intelligible. It is doubtful whether by itself it would ever have been completely popular. Something came to his aid which is much more popular than the love of satire : the profound and popular love of song. A genius in another school of art crossed his path and co-operated in his work ; giving wings to his words, and sending them soaring into the sky. Perhaps no other musician except Sullivan would have done it in exactly the right way ; would have been in exactly the right degree frivolous and exactly the right degree fastidious. A certain fine unreality had to hang over all the fantasies ; there was nothing rowdy, there was nothing in the special sense even rousing about such song, as there is in a serious, patriotic, or revolutionary song, or even drinking song. Everything must be seen in a magic mirror, a little more delicately distorted than the mirror of Shalott ; there must be no looking out directly upon passing events. The satiric figures were typical but not topical. All that precise degree of levity and distance from reality seemed to be expressed, as nothing else could express it, in the very notes of the music ; almost, one might say, in the note of the laughter that followed it. And it may be that in the re-mote future that laughter will still be heard, when all the voices of that age are silent.

G. K. CHESTERTON.

AUTHOR'S FOREWORD

THIS book presumes some knowledge on the reader's part of Gilbert and Sullivan Opera. It deals only indirectly with the historical or production side of the plays. Its aim is rather to treat them analytically, to note points of interest in their structure and in their characters, and to suggest new lines of study.

Gilbert and Sullivan has no small library already. My own addition to it may claim, worthily or otherwise, to have a two-fold justification. One reason is that the popular interest in these operas is growing rather than waning with the passing of years. The other is that this is an attempt, probably the first of its kind, to examine them as a whole, and from distinctive angles. If it is an appreciation—and that is admitted—it is also a critical appreciation. At the same time the criticism is light. It would be more than foolish to apply the sterner standards of judgment to such elfin and fanciful things. It would show, indeed, that one had missed the spirit of them, and that one was thus writing without understanding.

The chapters are in the main self-contained.

And because they are meant to be self-contained there may be some repetition and some over-lapping. A few of them appeared in the first instance in the columns of the " Gilbert and Sullivan Journal." For the liberty to reproduce them, usually in an amended and amplified form, I have sought, Pooh-Bah fashion, the permission of the Editor. He has never been known to deny me anything.

I have drawn, of course, on the common stock of knowledge regarding these operas, but references have been given scrupulously whenever possible. So far as I may have been remiss in this matter I tender to my creditors both apologies and acknow-ledgments. My quotations from the text, used as a rule for illustrative purposes only, have been taken from Messrs. Macmillan's admirable collected edition of the plays, " The Savoy Operas."

A. H. G.

CONTENTS

CONTENTS

GILBERT AND SULLIVAN

CHAPTER I

OVERTURE

GILBERT and Sullivan is one of the outstanding examples of partnership genius. Neither of the men who created it was a genius himself, but the association of the two, a gifted dramatist with a gifted composer, gave the world an art-form that has undeniable genius. There is nothing quite so perfect in its own sphere as Gilbert and Sullivan Opera. As a collaborative effort in humour and music it admits of no equal. It is so homogeneous, so closely woven into a single piece, that it might have sprung from one mind and from one inspiration.

The plays are not the work of a dramatist who retained a musician to set his lyrics or of a composer who worked on the material which an indifferent librettist provided. Neither Gilbert nor Sullivan was the superior partner. Without one another they were men who would have made no supreme reputation. In association they have linked their names imperishably as servants of the public's

I

happiness. Each complemented the other and drew the best out of the other in quite a remarkable way. The dramatist brought cleverness to the partnership and the composer brought beauty. And yet there is beauty also in Gilbert's work and cleverness in Sullivan's.

Gilbert and Sullivan has taken its place amongst the classic things of the stage. It is classic despite the fact that it is essentially popular in its form and in its appeal. Its " public " is said to number three million people. If there are three millions who are familiar with these delightful plays, who find enchantment in their wealth of wit and melody, and whose hearts are warmed by their gracious and enlivening spirit, there are things in them that deserve appreciative appraisement. They deserve it all the more because, as we shall see later, these comic operas are English of the English. They are English in their sentiment, in their outlook on life, and in their humorous and musical forms. And as a native product, racy of the soil and owing nothing at all to exotic influences, they are worth preserving as a treasured heritage.

The great feature of these works is their rhythmical elegance. No two words could more fittingly characterise Gilbert and Sullivan Opera. It is this rhythmical elegance, alike on the creative and interpretative sides, which has placed them in a class apart. It is the root-cause also of their enduring popularity. Gilbert himself was a great verbal rhythmist. In his lyrics his rhythmical or metrical adroitness is sometimes exceptional, and there is rhythm, too, in not a little of his dialogue. And his forms are certainly elegant. If we translate the word into refinement or tastefulness, we have the best definition we could possibly have of his humour, his literary style, and his stagecraft. Sullivan in his turn was unquestionably a great musical rhythmist. The charm of his music lies in its unfailing rhythm and its abounding melody. And the melody itself is always elegant. Whatever the defects of his music—and that is a matter we shall have to consider—its refinement and tastefulness cannot be questioned.

In all peoples the response to rhythm is an instinctive impulse. A great deal of modern popular music is intensely rhythmical. But most certainly it is not elegant. Sullivan's music has this life-giving rhythm, but it has also the melodic elegance which alone redeems rhythm, uncontrolled and unrestrained, from being barbaric and ugly. It is the same with the plays. They have humour and animation, and they necessarily have them, but these factors alone would not distinguish them from the common traffic of the stage. In addition they have a dignity and a reposefulness which the wider world has very largely forgotten. Certainly it has forgotten it if one must judge by the cacophony and jerkiness of the contemporary popular stage. There is about them an old-world charm and courtliness that make them increasingly precious survivals in a feverish age.

3

The plays are restful things in a restless generation. They are care-free in a world grown over-
anxious and weary. They take us out of our own
matter-of-fact environment and make us for a while
the observers of their own land of fantastic illusion.
And in this land of mirth and melody we meet
many whimsical people. They are very mannerly
people. In demeanour and speech they display a
faultless elegance. They are addicted to frankness,
they have a fondness for experiment, and they are
guided by their own code of logic. They are naïve
and simple people who have lighted somehow on
the true and only philosophy. With them " all's
as right as right can be." Possibly there is more
wisdom than we credit in their cheerful inconsequence and their resolute belief in that slogan.

Sir William Gilbert, who was the son of a retired
naval surgeon, is said to have written his first play
when a schoolboy at Ealing.[1] It was a " thriller,"
and he filled the triple rôle of author, scenic artist,
and actor. The plays he wrote, musical and non-
musical, numbered in all no fewer than seventy.
If the Crimean War had lasted a few weeks longer—
and there is scope for profound reflection in this
—he would probably have obtained a commission
and found his career in the Army. A Civil Service

[1] William Schwenck Gilbert was born at 17 Southampton Street,
Strand, on November 18, 1836, and died at Grim's Dyke, near Harrow,
on May 29, 1911, aged 75. Gilbert's end was heroic. He was bathing
with two young ladies in the lake in his own grounds. One of them
was in difficulties and he went to her rescue. He sank under her, the
circumstances pointing to heart failure, and not actually to drowning.

clerkship in an "ill-organised and ill-governed office" proved uncongenial to him, and within four years he had used part of an unexpected legacy to qualify himself for the legal profession, only to find its scanty rewards a new test on his patience. It was as a briefless barrister anxious to supplement his income that he took up the pen. When twenty-five he became associated with *Fun*. And it was on that lively little journal that he really laid the foundations of his fame on the stage. For it was to the columns of *Fun*, side by side with a good deal of miscellaneous writing, that he contributed the inimitable Bab Ballads, and it was these gay verses that were the practice ground of Gilbert and Sullivan Opera.

It is with the Bab Ballads that any study of the operas is bound to begin. Here it was that Gilbert sketched out his world of make-believe, turned the odd into the ordinary, and called it Topsy-Turvy-dom. In these nonsense verses, which have since been collected and reproduced with his own quaint illustrations, there is a sheer riot of imaginative gaiety. Some of the ideas he used later, but the spirit of all of them, elfish and infinitely fanciful, went into the plays. There is no material difference between the Gilbert of the Bab Ballads and the Gilbert of " H.M.S. Pinafore " and " The Mikado." So far as there is a difference at all, it is that of the apprentice who has become the master-hand, for-feiting just a little of his youthful exuberance, and making his satire a trifle more pointed.

Sir Arthur Sullivan was six years his partner's junior.[1]   In his case there was never any doubt as to the direction in which his career would be shaped. He was a military bandmaster's son, born and bred in a musical atmosphere, and destined quite early to be a composer.   Before he met Gilbert he had written a great deal of music, ranging from an oratorio and a symphony to hymns and songs, and it was probably his songs, prolific in their number, that gave him the best preparation for his later work on the light opera stage.   From the first he had an uncommon fund of melody, but it was the humorous satirist, who was no musician himself, who gave him the choicely polished lyrics that coaxed from him music of such infinite fancy and exquisite beauty.

Lucky was the coincidence of fortune that produced two such men in the same country and in the same generation.   By their alliance the national heart has ever since beat more joyously.   And yet the secret of their success has not been solely that their gifts were so complementary.   Gilbert and Sullivan, to begin with, never underrated their public's intelligence.   They discovered " what the public want " long before those words had been turned into a catch-phrase by small wits who conceive that the public want only inanity.   They realised that the need was for refreshing humour

[1] Arthur Seymour Sullivan was born at 8 Boswell Terrace, Lambeth, on May 13, 1842, and died at 1 Queen's Mansions in Victoria Street, S.W., on November 22, 1900, aged 58. He is buried in St. Paul's Cathedral.

6

and music, and that, if only the choice is available, the public prefer wholesome entertainment to verbal gibberish and musical shoddy. Gilbert's humour remains attractive because it is intelligent humour, because there is a liberal measure of it, because it is finely phrased, and because it never descends to commonplace claptrap. Sullivan's music remains attractive because it is genuinely tuneful and graceful. It never has the paucity, for instance, of the average musical comedy, which seems to be built around one sensuous waltz and a number of jingles.

Gilbert and Sullivan were in many respects opposites in character and temperament. But both men were artists. They knew how to use their resources tastefully and effectively. In particular they knew the best use to make of the chorus. A Gilbert and Sullivan chorus fills the rôle, like the classic chorus of old, of a commentator on the course of the story, and it is used always with a definite purpose. It is never introduced solely for the sake of parade. They knew also the value of attractive groupings. And they saw that each opera had an effective background. There is choiceness as well as novelty in their stage settings. For one of their scenes they have the Tower of London. For another they choose the exterior of the Houses of Parliament at Westminster. Operas there also are that charm the eye with a Venetian picture, with that of the palm groves of a languorous South Sea island, and with that of the bright colouring of old-time Japan. In all these scenes there is a tastefulness fully in accord with the elegant spirit of the plays.

They were men of ideas who reacted to each other sympathetically. And they were able to enforce their ideas without concessions or modifications to suit any third party. The fortunate circumstance that they were their own producers gave them a commanding position. Strictly speaking, it was Gilbert who was the producer, and there have been few authors who have been able to dictate so precisely how their stage works should be presented. He helped to select and he personally coached the players. He also laid down the traditions—the traditions which harmonise the lines of interpretation with the rhythmical elegance of the plays. Every detail had been carefully thought out beforehand, and the balance of the complete work of art which he and his partner had created was not to be disturbed by well-meaning artists, who were forbidden any textual digressions or interpolations. Nor in a Gilbert and Sullivan performance may there be any action or gesture which is not as free from every trace of vulgarity as the libretti and the music are conspicuously free. They have thus an artistic symmetry not usually found on the ordinary stage.

Gilbert has told us what was the early plan of campaign. In his speech at the O.P. Club dinner, which is often quoted from, he recalled that at the time the collaboration began English comic opera had practically ceased to exist, and that such musical entertainments as held the stage were adaptations of the plots of the operas of Offenbach, Audran, and Lecocq. The plots had been Bowdlerised out of intelligibility, and sometimes their treatment was frankly improper. " Sullivan and I set out with the determination to prove that these elements were not essential to the success of humorous opera. We resolved that our plots, however ridiculous, should be coherent; that our dialogue should be void of offence; and that on artistic principles no man should play a woman's part and no woman a man's. Finally, we agreed that no lady of the company should be required to wear a dress that she could not wear with absolute propriety at a private fancy-dress ball." In other words, their plays were to be intelligible and they were to be seemly, a courageous ideal in their own time, but one which has ever since done much for the health of the stage.

In the course of their history these operas have passed through two distinct phases. In their own day the humour was rather in advance of the public. When it was not too subtle it was too audacious. A certain judge found only a chastened pleasure in " Trial by Jury." He held that it was calculated to bring the Law into disrepute. " Iolanthe " offended a great newspaper because of its " gibes " —and with relief the writer announced that these had fallen flat !—at an institution that " many Englishmen admire and the rest are content to tolerate." Criticisms of this kind, which stood by

no means alone, probably reflected the wider per-
plexity of the age in this strange form of humour,
this irreverent phenomenon of Topsy-Turvydom.
It was " outrageous " and at the same time rather
intriguing. Each new play was awaited with eagerness so that it might be seen what fresh audacity it
would perpetrate. To-day there seems to be little
that is subtle or audacious in Gilbert and Sullivan.
In this second phase, partly because of familiarity,
and partly because of a broader sense of humour,
we find the plays enjoyable and not at all startling.
" G. and S." has become itself an institution that
" many Englishmen admire and the rest (presumably
the high-brows) are content to tolerate."

I must add a few words of explanation to this
introductory chapter. Gilbert objected to the
description of himself as a " playwright." [1] He
held that the word had a mechanical sound, and
that a dramatic writer should not be bracketed, as it
were, with a painstaking artisan like a wheelwright,
a millwright, or a shipwright. A novelist is not
called a " novelwright " or a painter a " picture-
wright." It is as a dramatist, therefore, that we
must describe him, even though we may not
ordinarily associate a dramatist with the sphere of
such light and fantastic comedy.

[1] When Gilbert received the accolade in 1907, he was described on
the official list as " Mr. William Gilbert, playwright." The objection
referred to was contained in a letter to a friend, and it will be found in
Dark and Grey's *W. S. Gilbert: His Life and Letters.* In another
letter he called his knighthood " a tin-pot, twopenny-halfpenny sort
of distinction, but as no dramatic author as such ever had it for dramatic
authorship alone, I felt I ought not to refuse it."

CHAPTER II

AN OPERATIC REVIEW

I DO not propose in this book to deal with the operas in any chronological sequence. It may be well, therefore, first of all to pass them in rapid review, to note their leading characters, and to give the very briefest outlines of their plots. From this we may proceed to consider them and those who wrote them from particular standpoints. They number thirteen—the " baker's dozen." Actually the first collaborative effort of Gilbert and Sullivan was " Thespis." The Olympians, grown old and effete, seek a renewal of youth by exchanging places for a time with a troupe of strolling players, but with disastrous results. The gods can no more adapt themselves to this workaday world than the Thespians can adapt themselves to Olympus. It was a Gilbertian theme, and the moral of it, that departures from the established order are fatal, was equally typical. This extravaganza, with Toole and Nellie Farren in the cast, was produced in 1871 under John Hollingshead's direction at the Gaiety. It ran only a month—it deserved a better fate— and the score has never been published. Hollingshead lost faith in the play. Someone was to profit from what to him was a tragic lack of prevision.

"Thespis," however, has been banished from the elect circle for a long number of years, and the reason for its excommunication is simple. It alone, of all these works, was the one which Richard D'Oyly Carte [1] never handled, and it was this same Richard D'Oyly Carte, infrequently though his name will figure in these records, who was the real father of Gilbert and Sullivan Opera. It was this shrewd man, a writer of undistinguished operetta before he turned to business and became a successful dramatic and musical agent, who saw the lodestone glinting amidst the ruins of "Thespis." He saw it more plainly when, as manager of the Royalty Theatre, he was more directly associated with the two men in the production of "Trial by Jury." Gilbert was already a popular dramatist of some reputation. Sullivan had already won a name as a tuneful composer. And these two plays had given evidence of an extraordinary complementary genius. He saw that there were potentialities that must be encouraged. Gilbert and Sullivan had to be induced to join forces in a more permanent way, and he was ready to found a company to finance the venture, to make all the plans, and to take a lease of the old Opera Comique.[2] The fulfilment of

[1] Richard D'Oyly Carte, who was also a Londoner by birth, was born on May 3, 1844, and died on April 3, 1901. In his earlier days he arranged the concerts or lecture tours of, amongst others, Mario, Oscar Wilde, and Stanley. He left £240,000, or more than double Gilbert's fortune and more than four times Sullivan's.

[2] This was in Wych Street, now obliterated by that more modern thoroughfare, Aldwych.

this scheme was a matter of time. Actually it came into being with " The Sorcerer."

Certainly it was due to Carte's faith, to his sure instinct as an impresario, and even more to his pertinacity, that the famous partnership, so productive in popular enjoyment, came into being. We do not know whether it was his intention to give Gilbert and Sullivan plays exclusively at the Opera Comique. We do know that, although there were some anxious times to begin with, there was never occasion for him to look elsewhere. He, indeed, was not only the founder of this operatic enterprise, but the hidden genius, the shrewd business head, that guided it in the old Wych Street building, and later housed it at the Savoy. He did not concern himself very much—he had no reason to—with the actual work of the stage. In the early days particularly he had troubles enough. Never was a man more afflicted with such an unreasonable board of directors. They were getting a handsome return on their outlay, but they put their own estimate on success, they were alarmed at the sight of a few empty seats, they had novel ideas about the opening and closing of the theatre, and they were severely critical of the management. During the run of " H.M.S. Pinafore " they sent vans to the theatre and tried to remove the scenery. Carte had to endure much before he could clear them out and have the lease renewed to himself. In a sense he was doubly lucky. He became master of his own household, and incidentally of the finances, just when the great popularity of the operas began.[1]

I must now return to " Trial by Jury." The subject of this one-act operetta is a breach of promise case, the setting one of the courts of justice, and the treatment a delightful travesty of legal proceedings. Edwin, a man of fickle tastes, has deserted his Angelina. In extenuation of his conduct, he declares that he is only obeying nature's laws, for nature is constantly changing. The Judge, who philanders first of all with one of the bridesmaids, and then with the jilted bride herself, precedes the hearing of the case with a rollicking biographical song.[2] This describes how, when a young barrister, he found a way to success by courting a rich attorney's elderly, ugly daughter. Counsel for the Plaintiff tells of honeyed hours between the couple that had made Camberwell a bower and Peckham an Arcadian vale. The Defendant's offer to marry one love to-day if he may marry another to-morrow is rejected by counsel on the ground that " to marry two at once is burglaree." The faithless swain thereupon besmirches his own character with a view to mitigating the damages. The lady, on the other hand, makes a parade of her devotion, also with a view to enhancing the damages. In the end the Judge,

---

[1] The story is told in greater detail in Cellier and Bridgeman's *Gilbert, Sullivan, and D'Oyly Carte*, and in S. J. Adair Fitz-Gerald's *The Story of the Savoy Opera.*

[2] It is well to remember that this part was originated by Fred Sullivan, the composer's brother, and, but for his lamented death, he would probably have filled the rôles created by George Grossmith.

unable to reconcile the parties, throws his books and papers about, comes down into the court, and promises to marry the lady himself. This, he holds, demonstrates that, though his law is fudge, of beauty he's a judge. " And," chorus the impressionable jury, " a good judge too." " Trial by Jury," in its wealth of good spirit and whimsical fancy, is unquestionably a great little opera.

" The Sorcerer " was the successor to " Trial by Jury." It is an unequal play, little of the humour and few of the tunes being of any great merit, though the story marks the beginning of what we are to call later the equality comedy. Ploverleigh is celebrating the betrothal of Alexis, the Guardsman son of Sir Marmaduke Pointdextre, and Aline, the daughter of the Lady Sangazure. Seeing in love the source of every earthly joy, Alexis would have it break down all the artificial barriers of rank and wealth, age and beauty, tastes and temper. In support of these noble principles he arranges that the villagers at the festivities shall drink a love-potion concealed in a large tea-pot. It is obtained from John Wellington Wells, a dealer in magic and spells, and in a dramatic incantation the " sprites of earth and air, fiends of flame and fire " are summoned by the necromancer to the " dreadful deed inspire." The charm works very quickly. Every man who drinks the toast falls in love, irrespective of age or station, with the first woman he meets and finds his affection returned, and very soon the villagers, who have not been addicted to marrying, are asking for their bonds to be tied by the vicar, Dr. Daly. It stirs in this sentimental old bachelor, who has brewed his own tea and thus escaped the spell, his own " aching memory of the old, old days." So far has the mischief gone that the aristocratic Sir Marmaduke has fallen in love with the village pew-opener Mrs. Partlet, the Lady Sangazure dotes on John Wellington Wells, and Aline exhibits a passionate tenderness for Dr. Daly. The spell can be broken only by sacrificial rites to Ahrimanes. The sorcerer, melodramatic to the end, commits this act of self-immolation by disappearing amidst fire and brimstone, and the festivities resume as if nothing has happened.

" H.M.S. Pinafore," which came next, definitely established the success of Gilbert and Sullivan Opera. It was its music—its succession of rollicking nautical airs—that captured the public's ear after the opera's not-too-auspicious beginning. The scene is the quarter-deck of a battleship.[1] Captain Corcoran is one of the most polite and considerate of skippers, treating his crew as a band of brothers, and holding very loosely the reins of discipline customary in the British Navy. The *Pinafore* is visited by Sir Joseph Porter, K.C.B., a living example to all landsmen that, by sticking to one's

[1] The stage picture is that of the quarter-deck of the old H.M.S. *Queen*, one of the wooden walls that played their part at Trafalgar. For the revival of *H.M.S. Pinafore*, Gilbert had a model made of one-half of the ship, correct to the minutest detail, and later he had the forward end made also and the two joined together. This beautiful piece of handicraft, with its ornamental hull and its complicated rigging, is preserved at his old home, Grim's Dyke.

desk and never going to sea, one may rise to be the
ruler of the Queen's Navee. This First Lord is a
believer in the independence of the lower deck and
in the cultivation of polite manners and polite
language afloat. He has come, attended by his
sisters, his cousins, and his aunts, to claim the
hand of Corcoran's daughter, Josephine. She,
however, loves and is loved by the dreamy able-
seaman, Ralph Rackstraw, and their scheme for a
midnight elopement is overheard and betrayed by
a deformed and unpopular seaman, Dick Deadeye.
But when Corcoran surprises the lovers Rackstraw
openly avows his love and hurls his defiance as an
Englishman. In lusty tones he is acclaimed by
the crew :

> " For he might have been a Roosian,
> A French or Turk or Proosian
> Or perhaps Itali-an,
> But in spite of all temptations
> To belong to other nations
> He remains an Englishman."

In his wrath Corcoran utters an explosive word and
horrifies the First Lord of the Admiralty. He is
banished to his cabin in disgrace. Rackstraw, as a
presumptuous mariner, is also sent to the dungeon.
But then it is revealed by Little Buttercup, a
Portsmouth bumboat woman, that when she
practised baby farming she mixed up Corcoran and
Ralph Rackstraw. And promptly Rackstraw becomes the captain of the *Pinafore* and is pledged
to Josephine. Corcoran, degraded into a common

seaman, finds a life partner, oddly enough in the circumstances, in Little Buttercup.

" The Pirates of Penzance " has a melodramatic theme turned topsy-turvy. The pirates are too tender-hearted to make piracy pay. In particular, as orphans themselves, they make a point of never molesting an orphan, and the last three ships they took proved, unluckily for them, to be manned entirely by orphans. Frederic, who was meant to be a pilot, and by an alliterative error became a pirate instead, is just completing his apprenticeship, and he threatens that henceforward he must apply himself heart and soul to their extermination. They agree that he must do whatever his conscience dictates. Major-General Stanley—the type of military man who knows no more of tactics than a novice in a nunnery—has a large family of daughters. When they visit the pirates' cove they are captured. But the gang's visions of the " felicity of unbounded domesticity " are shattered when the father declares that he is an orphan. It was a lie, of course, and the old general broods over it and humbles himself before the tombs of his ancestors, who are his ancestors only by purchase. Frederic, meanwhile, has organised an expedition of police to capture the pirates, though they have to be spurred on by Mabel, one of the daughters, to " go to glory, though they die in combat gory." But before this mission commences the King of the Pirates and Ruth, the maid-of-all-work, announce to Frederic that he was born in a leap year, that he has had only five birthdays, and that he is thus still an apprentice, a position which he accepts loyally as " a slave of duty." Not only does he accept it, but he dutifully discloses that Major-General Stanley was not an orphan and that he has, in the King's words, practised on the pirates' " credulous simplicity." In the fight between the police and the pirates the police are defeated, but the prostrate sergeant calls on the victors to yield in Queen Victoria's name, a claim on their allegiance which they cannot resist. For these pirates, it transpires, are not members of the common throng, but noblemen who have all gone wrong.

"Patience" is a deliberate satire on the aesthetic craze of the 'eighties. Burnand's " The Colonel " had already made play with the same subject, but a foot-note to the programme indicated, though without specifically stating it, that the opera was completed before the farce had appeared. In any case it owed its forerunner nothing. Burnand's treatment was a plain grotesque. Gilbert and Sullivan, on the other hand, showed aestheticism "idealised." It was, of course, a more refined and a cleverer method, and it has clearly proved more enduring. Bunthorne is said to have been modelled on Oscar Wilde and Grosvenor (this is a more debatable matter) on Swinburne. Patience, a village milk-maid, is loved by the two poets, but she has only a subsidiary place in the story. It deals rather with the vanities of Bunthorne, a poseur afflicted with a morbid love of admiration, and the adorations of the twenty love-sick maidens, his aesthetic disciples. In their forlorn hope these classic figures are banded together in a sisterhood of misery. Bunthorne, a self-convicted sham, encounters a rival in Grosvenor. The new-comer, whose life's mission it is to reveal his physical perfection for the delectation of his fellow-creatures, is as placid and as insipid as the other is " highly spiced." He becomes, nevertheless, the new object of rapture, and the women discard Bunthorne for him as they had previously deserted their old sweethearts in the Dragoon Guards. By melodramatic means Bunthorne induces Grosvenor to change his appearance and become commonplace. The women, however, change with him, and the egotist is left in aesthetic isolation, consoled only by " a poppy and li-ly." " Patience " is a charming play despite its faded subject. During its run it was transferred from the Opéra-Comique to the new Savoy Theatre. And all the works, including the five not actually produced here, have been identified ever since as the Savoy Opera.

" Iolanthe " introduces us to Fairyland—or a little of Fairyland and a little of Old Palace Yard at Westminster. This is probably the cleverest opera. The satire is delicious, the fanciful idea is handled with remarkable smoothness, and the music is rich in the daintiest melody. Iolanthe was once the life and soul of Fairyland. She wrote its songs and arranged its dances, but many years ago she had married a mortal, a lapse that had placed her outside the fairy pale. When she is recalled from banishment, most of it spent at the bottom of a well, it is revealed that she has a son, the Arcadian shepherd Strephon. He is half fairy, half mortal, an inconvenient form of existence, inasmuch as his body can creep through keyholes, but not his legs. Among the Lord Chancellor's wards is Phyllis, a shepherdess whose charms have " powerfully affected " the Peers, and in order that the Lord Chancellor may award her to the Noble Lord whom he may select, the House hold an informal session in Arcady. Phyllis, however, resolves to " stick to her pipes and her tabors," and rejects Lord Tolloller and Lord Mountararat, because she is to be married to Strephon. When this disobedience to an order of the court threatens to separate the lovers for ever, the Queen of the Fairies takes Strephon under her protection, and sends him to represent one of her pocket boroughs in Parliament. In the next scene, a picture of Old Palace Yard by moonlight, we meet that delightful sentry-philosopher, Private Willis. The Peers are in a tantrum because, like a Parliamentary Pickford, Strephon " carries everything." The Lord Chancellor, after wrestling with himself, discovers that with legal propriety he may marry his own ward, Phyllis. Then Iolanthe addresses him. She pleads for her son, and she reveals to the Lord Chancellor, moreover, that she is his wife and he the father of Strephon. And it is soon revealed also that the Fairies have married the Peers. That by the fairy law means death, but the dilemma is solved by revising the law, so that a fairy who does *not* marry a mortal must perish. And in the end the Peers take wing and fly with the Peris " up in the sky ever so high."

" Princess Ida," the one three-act work of the series, is based on an earlier Gilbert non-musical play, described as a " respectful perversion " of Tennyson. Like " The Princess " itself, this is a satire on the feminist movement, and it bears the marks of age. King Gama, a " twisted monster all awry," comes with his three warrior sons to the court of King Hildebrand. With him should also have been his daughter, betrothed in infancy to Hilarion, but she has secluded herself in a Women's University. She and her students have renounced mankind and their rules are rigorous. Hilarion and his friends scale the walls of her retreat at Castle Adamant. They have dressed themselves as girl graduates, but their ruse is discovered, and they are arrested and bound by the Daughters of the Plough. Hildebrand and his soldiers meanwhile storm the castle gates. They bring Gama with them as hostage. He sees his daughter, and this meddlesome misanthropist tells her that in his captivity he is suffering tortures worse than death, inasmuch as he is given everything he needs and is denied all occasion for grumbling. In compassion for him Ida allows the soldiers to enter. Gama's three sons, having divested themselves of their armour, are vanquished in combat with Hilarion, Florian and Cyril. Princess Ida sees the ruin of her scheme to make her womenfolk abjure tyrannic man and renews her vows to Hilarion. The opera contains delightful music, but the story is not a good one for the dramatist's style, and as a subject for satire it has lost its piquancy.

With "The Mikado" we come to one of the greatest of the plays. Here the scene is Japan. Ko-Ko, an ex-tailor, has been liberated from jail, to which he had been confined for flirting, and installed in the office of Lord High Executioner. Pooh-Bah, an avaricious noble of immensely ancient lineage, is Lord High Everything Else. Nanki-Poo, the heir to the throne, has fled his father's court rather than marry the elderly Katisha, and in the disguise of a second trombone player he has fallen in love with Ko-Ko's ward and fiancée, Yum-Yum. Ko-Ko has incurred the Imperial displeasure and the risk of losing his own head because there have been no executions in Titipu. In his search for a victim he finds Nanki-Poo, disconsolate that Yum-Yum cannot be his wife and ready to end an unendurable existence, and the bargain is struck that he shall marry the girl for a month if he will then consent to be " beheaded handsomely." Later Ko-Ko and Pooh-Bah concoct a graphic story of the execution that is supposed to have taken place, and this is offered to the Mikado, a despot whose " object all sublime " it is to " make the punishment fit the crime." It is disclosed that they have encompassed the death of no other than the Heir-Apparent. In the Mikado's code this offence is to be expiated by a form of death that is " lingering, with either boiling oil or melted lead," but the penalty is avoided when it is realised that Nanki-Poo is alive and married to Yum-Yum. And Ko-Ko has to take under his wing the " most unattractive old face " of Katisha.

" Ruddigore " has a not unattractive title—or not unattractive until the word is analysed. This title is the first thrust of satire in a play which is mainly a satire at the expense of the melodramatic traditions of places like the old Surrey. It has no " blood and thunder " itself, but it does have its wicked baronet, its simple village maiden, its breezy sailor-man home from the sea, all of them stock characters which could be relied upon to win the jeers and the cheers of the " gods." Here, of course, we have no more than mock melodrama, a satirical sub-structure for a bright and tuneful play. A heavy doom rests on the baronets of Ruddigore. They must commit a crime a day or perish. In order to escape this fate the last of the line had disappeared. He is disguised as Robin Oakapple, a young farmer with the manners of a Marquis and the morals of a Methodist, and his title and its curse have been inherited by his younger brother, Sir Despard Murgatroyd, whose enforced villainies have de-ranged his sweetheart, the crazy Mad Margaret. Robin, too shy to woo himself, invites his sailor foster-brother, Richard Dauntless, to woo for him by proxy the etiquette-loving young lady, Rose Maybud. So well does Richard do it that he wins her himself, and a curious kink of conscientiousness leads him, moreover, to betray his relative's secret to Sir Despard. Oakapple is thus forced to assume his baronet's rank and its evil heritage. For a week he makes faltering efforts to commit his crime every day, but he has to be spurred on by the visitation of the ancestral ghosts, ordinarily the oil paintings that adorn the picture gallery of Castle Ruddigore. Escaping their tortures only by promising to be faithful to his sorry destiny, he commits through his man-servant, Old Adam, a mistake that helps to break the evil spell for ever and to restore the last of the baronets, Sir Rhoderic, to life and to the hand and heart of his old sweetheart, Dame Hannah. Robin, a farmer again, marries Rose Maybud.

" The Yeomen of the Guard " is the one more serious work in the series. Gilbert and Sullivan have deserted satire, and they have given us a human and a moving story, improbable in some of its details, but nearer probability than most of the plots. It is unlike anything else they did, more delicate in its sentiment, more artistic and gracious in its appeal. There is humour in it, but there is the touch of sadness as well, and the laughter is never far removed from the sigh. The music, beautiful at all times, has a wistfulness, a restraint, not to be found in the other operas. It is not here that Sullivan's muse is joyous or sparkling. Most of his leading themes have a melancholy tinge, a sad and reflective note, which, nevertheless, never strikes very deeply. The scene is Tower Green, the period is the Tudor period, and the atmosphere is the atmosphere of old Merrie England. Actually, although the story deals with a time before Shakespeare, the language is often suggestive of Shakespeare. Jack Point is a figure not unrelated to Touchstone. He is a strolling player—a Merry-man of infinite wit—working the fairs in company with Elsie Maynard. For the sake of one hundred crowns he allows the girl to be married blindfold to the condemned Colonel Fairfax. In an hour's time that undaunted soldier of fortune is to be beheaded and she will regain her liberty. Sergeant Meryll and his daughter Phœbe, meanwhile, secure the prisoner's release by surreptitiously obtaining the keys from the dismal jailor, Wilfred Shadbolt. Jack Point realises too late his own love for Elsie Maynard. The girl has found happiness in the arms of her bridegroom in the strange adventure on Tower Green. Fate has cheated the jester, and he falls insensible, a tragic figure in motley, from heart-broken grief.

" The Gondoliers," which comes next in the order of production, is one of the brightest and most attractive of all the operas. A Spanish grandee, the impecunious Duke of Plaza-Toro, has arrived in Venice with his Duchess, his daughter Casilda, and his " suite," the drummer-boy Luiz. Casilda had been married by proxy as a baby to the Heir to the Baratarian Throne. All the Grand Inquisitor, the sedate Don Alhambra, can say about this young husband is that he is now plying the modest but picturesque calling of a gondolier. In his infancy, it appears, his identity had been mixed up with that of the son of a common Venetian citizen, but of one thing there is no possible, probable shadow of doubt, and that is that he is either Marco or Giuseppe. The Grand Inquisitor, having announced this fact to the Duke, announces also to Marco and Giuseppe, both of them ardent Republicans, that one of them is a King. Further, as Barataria is in a state of insurrection, it is needful that they should leave their young brides, sail over the seas, and wield the sceptre jointly. In the next scene the happy-go-lucky gondoliers have adopted their plan of a " Monarchy re-modelled on Republican principles." In this State every man, from the meanest to the highest, is equal. They receive a number of visitors. The Grand Inquisitor is disturbed by the sight of a system which throws all class distinctions into the melting-pot. They are re-united with Tessa and Gianetta, in honour of whose arrival a gay cachucha is danced, but the brides have to learn that one of the husbands, whoever he may be, was previously married and is thus an unintentional bigamist. And the Duke of Plaza-Toro, his fortunes restored by means of turning himself into a company, has reason to chide the regal gondoliers for not impressing their courtiers, and he gives them a lesson in the arts of deportment. The dilemma is soon cleared up. The Royal foster-mother is produced by the Grand Inquisitor, and she reveals that the rightful heir is neither Marco nor Giuseppe, but the drummer-boy Luiz, who has been all along the lover of Casilda.

" Utopia Limited " moves the scene once more to the lotus-land of the Southern Pacific.[1] Langour there may have been, but by no means dullness, in that remote country with its picturesque palm groves. King Paramount, a benevolent Monarch with a sense of humour, is in constant danger of being blown up by the Public Exploder. Scaphio and Phantis, members of the Utopian judiciary, maintain a tyrannous watch upon his Majesty, and they require him to chronicle his own improprieties in a scandalous organ, the " Palace Peeper." The Royal twins, Nekaya and Kalyba, are being transformed into typically bashful English maidens by their stern Mentor, Lady Sophy. The King's eldest daughter, the Princess Zara, is returning from Girton, and already there are stirrings on the part of the inhabitants to re-model their manners, customs and forms of government on those of that great and wise country England. Zara brings with her, in addition to Captain FitzBattleaxe and his Guardsmen, five other Flowers of Progress. They are the " types of England's power, a heaven-enlightened band " by whose guidance Utopia is

---

[1] *Utopia* healed the breach that had occurred between Gilbert and Sullivan after *The Gondoliers*. It was, as regards these two men, in no sense a quarrel. Gilbert, interposing in a managerial detail which did not properly concern him, objected to the expenditure on a foyer carpet by D'Oyly Carte. It was a trivial matter in itself, but it developed acrimoniously, and Sullivan, compelled at last to take sides with one of his partners, supported D'Oyly Carte.

to be reorganised and "completely Anglicized." A beginning is made when Mr. Goldbury, a company promoter, explains how one may float the rashest venture on very little capital, and if one succeeds " your profits are tremendous " and if one fails " bang goes your eighteen pence." The King argues that, while it seems rather dishonest, what is good enough for England, the greatest commercial country in the world, is good enough for Utopia, and he becomes the first monarch in Christendom to register his Crown under the Joint Stock Companies' Act. Henceforward, by ruling the country through a board of directors, he is able to defy Scaphio and Phantis. But all the reforms have only stifled progress. Something, it seems, has been omitted, and that is the introduction of party government, that " bulwark and foundation of England's greatness." Once again there will be general and unexampled prosperity. And when we part with the Utopians in this delightful satirical play they are singing their hymn of homage to England.

" The Grand Duke " brings the end to this rapid survey. In all truth the work was a fatal thirteenth. It is the last, and indisputably it is the worst, of the operas. It had the shortest run, it has never been revived, and no good service will be done to the collaborators if it is withdrawn from its obscurity. Gilbert's humour has descended to the level of the sausage-roll. The munching of a sausage-roll is the sign and countersign for the conspirators. The opera itself is littered with false rhymes. Sullivan's music has also fallen to the tin-pot tunes, few of them, apart from the opening wedding chorus, being other than unex-hilarating and undistinguished. The scene this time is that of a German Grand Duchy of Pfennig-Halbpfennig. The chief theme is that of the so-called statutory duel, according to which the parties to a quarrel draw cards, the rival who selects the lower card is to be considered socially dead, and the winner is compelled to " adopt the loser's poor relations, discharge his debts, pay all his bets, and take his obligations." By these means a bloodless revolution serves to dethrone the Grand Duke Rudolph, a poor creature obsessed by etiquette and half-pence, in favour of a troupe of Thespians, headed by Ludwig. The plot is tedious and in-volved. In the end the tangle is unravelled by the discovery of an unexpected clause in the Duel Act. This makes the ace the lowest card of all, and the discovery is sufficient to send the theatrical court, who have dressed as Athenians, back to the theatre, and to restore Rudolph, who has discarded his Baroness and marries a daughter of the Prince of Monte Carlo.

I have described the stories in their briefest outlines only, but the operas have been dealt with in their proper sequence, and in the pages that follow they are to be discussed without reference to the order in which they were introduced to the public.

CHAPTER III

HERALDS OF THE RENAISSANCE

I HOLD—though my seniors may gravely upbraid me for it—that Gilbert and Sullivan was the heartiest thing that came out of the Victorian Age. It is one of the Victorian institutions most worth preserving. And it represents a landmark in theatrical history. The English stage as it was before Gilbert and Sullivan was vastly different from what it was after Gilbert and Sullivan. We may not give the operas the whole credit for the salutary change. We cannot deny them some of the credit. They were the heralds of a better and a brighter order in the world of the stage. They gave heartiness where there had been dullness, refinement where there had been crudeness, a waft of intelligence where there had been banality. They also made the English stage once again essentially English.

Any description of the state of the theatre in those times makes dreary reading. English dramatic art, with all the wonderful traditions that it had behind it, was in the grip of a foreign stranglehold. It was the age of clumsy adaptation. An

authoritative and trenchant critic has told us the
story.[1]   For years the stage had been overrun with
French operettas of the school of Offenbach.   In
the land of their origin these may have been graceful
enough.   In their translated form they were utterly
devoid alike of dramatic ingenuity and literary
quality.   " They had been hastily adapted," says
the writer, " by slovenly hacks, and their librettos,
often witty in the original, became farragos of
metreless doggerel and punning ineptitude."   He
adds that the reaction began in 1875 with the
performance at the Royalty Theatre of " Trial by
Jury."

The British playwright of the period had seemed
to be unable to raise his mind above these exotic
adaptations.   It was held to be his normal occupation.   He was distrustful of, probably himself
downright deficient in, originality.   The public was
content to take what it was given.   The standard of
taste was at its lowest.   It was satisfied with a sort
of burlesque that was usually vulgar and pointless.
It was ready to applaud the coarse woman in tights.
It did not ask that a play should have sense, any
form or coherence, or any link whatever with
reality.   Lecocq, Offenbach, Planquette, and other
Frenchmen supplied the spicy tunes, and the
dialogue and situations with which the parodists
linked these tunes together were just an unintelligible
jumble.

[1] See article on the Drama, initialled A. W. W., in the *Encyclopædia
Britannica*.

This was the condition of the theatre in the middle of the nineteenth century. It is not surprising that the play-going public was rather a minor quantity. It was held, and perhaps with some warrant, that the theatre was no place for nicely bred people. So those of them in London who wanted to be amused struck a compromise with their consciences by going to a theatre that was not called a theatre in Lower Regent Street. Here were to be seen the German Reed Entertainments. They were "select" in tone, but most of the productions lumbered in the old, old rut of mediocrity. Gilbert did work for these entertainments in his apprenticeship days, and it was in the Reeds' Gallery of Illustration, long since demolished, that in 1870 he was first introduced to Sullivan by Frederick Clay, the composer best known to fame by his " I'll sing thee songs of Araby."

It would not be true to say that Gilbert and Sullivan first aroused the theatre out of its stupor. The Renaissance was due, and it would have come about without them, though they were in the forefront of the new movement and certainly helped it along. Signs of the revival had been seen already in the success of the so-called " cup and saucer comedy." Tom Robertson had begun to rattle the dry bones of the drama and infuse new life into its comatose body. The honour done to this man has been far less than his due. The public also had tired of the babbling inanities of the outworn burlesque. It wanted something better—

something that would pay a passing compliment to its intelligence.

Gilbert and Sullivan, it should be remembered, came on the scene under singular auspices. The Industrial Revolution half-a-century earlier had made the country prosperous. Cities and towns had sprung rapidly out of towns and villages under the stimulus of a rapidly growing urban population. The wider franchise laws had been in existence sufficiently long to broaden the popular interest in politics and general affairs. The abolition of the stamp duties had given the nation the enormous advantages of a cheap press. The sense of humour had been sharpened up. Everybody had been waiting eagerly for each new instalment of the " Pickwick Papers." Later on there came the biggest step forward in popular education that there has ever been in the country. The Education Act of 1870 was passed a mere five years before the production of " Trial by Jury." And the zest for knowledge had been furthered by the mechanics' institutes and the old " penny readings."

The public was thus a better educated and a more alert public. It had also commenced to disentangle itself from the meshes of conventionality. This was to prove a long process. The theatre-going habit had still to be developed. Gilbert and Sullivan had many things in their favour when they began, but what they did not have was a ready-made public or a public, to put it more precisely, that accepted the theatre without questionings or misgivings as

34

one of the great recreative agencies. They made their following rapidly, and in so far as they made the stage morally wholesome and intellectually fresher, and in that way more widely acceptable, they helped materially in the creation of the present great play-going public. It was not the least of their achievements.

If we look back to the earlier English dramatists, and if we try to find the one to whom Gilbert may be most closely compared, it is probable that our choice will be Congreve. The gulf of time between the two men was a wide one, and it is bound to account, of course, for many differences in dramatic form and technique. Congreve was a great satirist, and his comedies have literary quality, his dialogue is well written, his humour is now and then of the saturnine kind, and his thrusts at the liberties of his time, while pointed, are hardly vituperative or scathing. In most of these directions Gilbert can be classed as his descendant. Congreve's characters are usually very unpleasant people. If many of his men are knaves, if many of his women are women of the world, we may or may not accept them as faithful types of his generation. Gilbert's characters, on the other hand, are almost exasperatingly pleasant. They have, nevertheless, the harmless foibles and amiable weaknesses of the real men and women of our own time, and we can identify them readily.

Gilbert's " father " in theatrical matters was without a doubt Tom Robertson, the author of such laconically named plays as "Ours," "Caste," and "Society." And yet he was only one of the sons in a very large family. Nearly all the late Victorian and modern drama traces back a more or less direct line to the same "progenitor." It was Robertson who first lifted the theatre out of the doldrums and the ruts of degeneracy. It was he who, while keeping strictly to the sphere of comedy, showed how plays should have contact with the realities, how they should be peopled with living types, and how they should be affected by serious thought. Up to that time the silly burlesques had admitted none of these things. They were as remote from life as possible. The " cup and saucer " school was so called because of its fondness for the homely details and domestic settings. The " realism " of it was rather startling in that generation. A dramatist who used a middle-class parlour for his stage picture was so distinctive that he had to be labelled and badged.

It was Robertson also—as a rule we overlook this—who was the first of the real stage managers. He had, unlike any other man of his time, a flair for the stage. He realised that a play should be something more than a recital of dull dialogue before a dull background. He knew his players, he knew what they could do, and he knew what could be contrived in the way of movement and by-play. He also studied his stage picture. It was, as we have seen, usually a homely picture, not at all ornate, but it certainly helped the atmosphere. He studied also the grouping of the characters and all the other major and minor details of effective production. Gilbert attended many of Robertson's rehearsals, and not only did he learn much from them, which he admitted, but what he learnt was the basis of his own greater stagecraft.

The English stage has moved on since Robertson's time, but it should not be unmindful of the debt it owes to him, coupled with interpreters like the Kendals and the Bancrofts. Gilbert, who came immediately after him, necessarily comes closest to him in style. It was not, however, a case of imitation. Gilbert could rival Robertson in his sureness of stagecraft, in his fund of ingenious and wholesome humour, and in his gift of bright and natural dialogue writing. He was not, on the other hand, quite so true a delineator of human character, and the realities of life and its problems, which in Robertson we meet " face to face," in Gilbert we see, as it were, " through a glass darkly."

Both men were Victorian in their sentiment, often a veneer for cynicism, as well as in their prejudice. It has been said of Robertson that, while he is ready enough to depict the follies of rank and the absurdities of the newly rich, his main doctrine is that " the classes should never mingle, that the working man should learn to stay in his appointed place, and that the bourgeoisie should have no yearnings to intrude into the often-impoverished drawing-rooms and libraries of Aristocrat Castle." [1]

[1] Allardyce Nicholl in *British Drama*.

That, of course, was Gilbert's own outlook on life, and it was the theory which, as we shall see later, he loved to thrust home by his own process of turning it topsy-turvy.

Gilbert and Sullivan is in essence a late survival of what has been known as the Comedy of Manners. It was also a fore-runner of the Drama of Ideas, not because it claimed an intellectual basis itself, but because it served as the medium of transition from a discredited theatrical form to the drama written with intellectual vigour and a serious purpose. It " substituted original invention for parody and the wanton degradation and vulgarisation of historic or legendary themes, it set up a very high standard of versification in the lyric numbers, and it substituted polished prose for the doggerel dialogue of the old burlesques, bristling with idiotic puns." [1] And by these means, to summarise the writer whom I am quoting, it did undeniably " restore literary self-respect to the English stage."

Self-respect was restored to it, indeed, for one other reason, and that was that the English stage became once again English. French opera bouffe had been driven out of the field. In a sense it had been beaten at its own game. Sullivan had little to fear from the Offenbach school, and Gilbert himself was a giant beside the feeble wits who had been trimming too long that dreary glimmer, the so-called " sacred lamp of burlesque." It was snuffed out with ridiculous ease.

[1] William Archer in *Real Conversations*.

CHAPTER IV

THE ENGLISHMAN'S LOOKING-GLASS

THE Englishman's amiable failings provide the great stock-pot of ideas for the Gilbert and Sullivan Opera. Gilbert traded upon national idiosyncrasies very adroitly. The Englishman is pictured, not as the envious foreigner sees him, often a gross and perfidious creature, but as he might see himself through a looking-glass. The image is complimentary rather than flattering. Gilbert, as we shall see later, was a master of paradox who was himself a paradox, but this merely proves him to have been true to his nationality.

For, now we come to it, what is the Englishman but a bundle of contradictions, a living enigma to the bewildered foreigner? He is a mixture of hard sense and sentiment. He is a plain citizen who has nevertheless an affection for titles and the social ornamentations. He is an easy-going fellow who has a knack of forging ahead of his rivals. He is by instinct a non-intellectual person who has a fund of the shrewdest intelligence. He clings to a vague conviction that he is the salt of the earth and a far from vague conviction that he is eternally going to the dogs.

39

GILBERT AND SULLIVAN

Perhaps the Englishman's greatest virtue is that he has never taken himself too solemnly. In his sanity, in his genius for keeping an even keel in smooth weather and rough, lies his essential strength. He is conscious of his follies and futilities, he sees them mirrored before his eyes in these operas, and he enjoys the joke hugely. It is at his own reflection that the good fellow is laughing. For let us never doubt that, whatever the merits or otherwise of the Gilbert and Sullivan characters as dramatic figures, they are usually of the genre of the common, everyday Englishman. The passing of time may have lent some modifications, but in the more permanent elements in the national type, more particularly the ridiculous ones, these characters make some approach to reality.

First of all is that curious habit of self-disparagement. Study the first lines of all the big parts in the operas, and you will see that the characters, with a quite remarkable frankness, invariably belittle themselves and disclaim any real talents or accomplishments. You know the worst about them from the beginning. You realise afterwards that, while these people are not usually an intellectual lot, their candour did them less than justice. You observe, moreover, that it is typical of them that they take their troubles light-heartedly, and certainly never tragically. In these respects they are English. It is the Englishman's sense of humour that has saved him again and again in a crisis.

I think we may view the operas from one other

aspect. The story in many of them turns on some extravagant social or political experiment. It is a theme that is bound to appeal to the humorous faculty of the Englishman. He is ever a believer in the *status quo*. He is evolutionary—and even that at his own orderly pace—but never revolutionary. Sweeping changes in forms of government or in the social order he has always regarded as something of a joke. The political theorist is disheartened again and again by his devastating sanity. And the Englishman sees the joke of the thing—no one was ever calculated to see it better—when these plays give a free rein to fanciful theory.

One of the most downright English things in the operas—and you may substitute the word British all the time if you prefer it—is Lord Mountararat's song in " Iolanthe." The House of Peers' reference need not be too rigidly interpreted. It has a much wider application.

> " When Wellington thrashed Bonaparte,
>   As every child can tell,
>   The House of Peers, throughout the war,
>   Did nothing in particular,
>   And did it very well :
>   Yet Britain set the world ablaze
>   In good King George's glorious days !

> " And while the House of Peers withholds
>   Its legislative hand,
>   And noble statesmen do not itch
>   To interfere with matters which
>   They do not understand,
>   As bright will shine Great Britain's rays
>   As in King George's glorious days ! "

Jingoism never cloaked itself with such unaffected modesty. The song reflects the native gift for " muddling through."

Yet the most English of all the operas is " The Gondoliers." The people we see on the Piazzetta in Venice and in the Throne-room of some uncharted Ruritania are the people we may meet any day in Piccadilly. The historical costumes they wear, the old-world manners they imitate, are the thinnest disguise. No one would ever pretend that Don Alhambra is a typical Grand Inquisitor of Spain. He is just a plump, substantial, good-natured, level-headed, slow-moving Englishman. Sometimes he may seem a little stiff, but his outlook on life, his refusal to be stampeded, even his taste for platitudes, are uncommonly English. The Duke of Plaza-Toro, masquerading as a Spanish grandee, is (omitting his rather discreditable military past) clearly another Englishman. He belongs to the down-at-heel nobility, the old order which, impoverished though it may be, still holds itself proudly. He has, nevertheless, a shrewd business head and the gift, English like, of "adaptability." No one in this wide world would ever mistake him for a Spaniard. Certainly no one would make a similar mistake in regard to his Duchess. She is a grand lady of the old school and unquestionably English.

" The Gondoliers " has been described very often as a satire on snobbery. But why ? It is true that the courtiers have this defect. They have risen far above their station, and the wine has been heady. Neither Don Alhambra nor the Duke, though not deficient in the sense of his own importance, is obviously afflicted with snobbery. Still less do Marco and Giuseppe, to whom the story chiefly relates, suffer from the complaint. They are, to me, just a couple of natural, happy-go-lucky young Englishmen. A big adventure calls them over the seas, and because it is an adventure, and because they belong to the race of the old pioneers, they set out on it light-heartedly and gaily. The job they have to tackle does not appal them. They flounder into absurdities, and they flounder out of them again, and they extract from their novel situation any amount of fun and enjoyment. They remind one of high-spirited school-boys on a rollicking holiday.

Marco and Giuseppe were Venetian boatmen. Suppose we change the scene, turn them into London cabmen, and picture them called on to journey to a distant land to assume the orb and sceptre of an insurrectory State. In this form we see how diverting is the central theme of the opera. The London taxi-driver might do it—even if amidst his regal splendours he pined for his modest Pimlico home and for the chance to tootle his horn once again along Piccadilly. Marco and Giuseppe are decidedly English. They have the Englishman's love of adventure, his adaptability and levelheadedness, and his virtue of not taking himself too solemnly. Can you imagine what the story would have been had these youths been puffed up with pomp and insisted on the Divine Right of (even temporary) Kings?

Gilbert's satire is mainly of the looking-glass type. He invites us to see ourselves, not precisely as outsiders see us, but as we are seen " by one of the family." A more serious race would take the satire amiss. The Englishman accepts it because he has a sense of the ridiculous, because he realises that many of his own habits and treasured predilections are themselves ridiculous, and because he sees that the cap fits quaintly and not grotesquely. He knows that he is insular, that he is in many respects illogical, and that he makes a creed of self-depreciation. He also knows that, like many of the characters in these operas, he falls into comical scrapes, rarely gets flustered, and in some odd fashion " muddles through."

" England is the greatest, the most powerful, and the wisest country in the world," declares one of the Anglophiles in the lotus-land of Utopia. As a plain statement this does not seem to stray very far from platitude. And yet at the performances audiences have regarded it as one of the funny lines of the play. The compliments are " put on too thick " for the average Englishman. So far as it is irony—and probably the dramatist meant it for that—he can see the point of it and find it amusing. In a minor way it is a sidelight on national psychology.

The humour, the sentiment, and the music of

these plays are essentially English. Gilbert and Sullivan, indeed, belongs to the soil, and it has not, taken as a whole, transplanted very successfully. Except in the case of " H.M.S. Pinafore " and " The Mikado," and then most probably because of their music, it has had no great hold on the Continent. France, above all a logic-loving country, has never had much time for the operas. Germany has given a more kindly welcome to them, but to a sober-minded nation, not given unduly to levity, they have appeared a trifle bewildering. One could never imagine the Germans of the old school making mockery of their Army as Gilbert invites us to make pleasant mockery of the British House of Lords or the Navy.

In the United States a number of the operas, though not the entire circle, have flourished. The chief aim there has been, not the maintenance of the traditional lines of interpretation, which cannot be insisted upon, but the presentation of the works with most spectacular settings.[1] By these means it is sought to cover up deficiencies inevitable in a country which has few actors trained in the comic opera school and which has no permanent organisation for producing these operas. Many years ago " The Pirates of Penzance " enjoyed a rage that was almost epidemic. To-day the most successful works, not least with the amateur societies, are " The Mikado," " H.M.S. Pinafore," and

[1] In a recent revival of *H.M.S. Pinafore* in New York a full Marines' Band played on the stage.

"Patience." "The Gondoliers," on the other hand, has never taken firm root in a land which has little use for social distinctions, and in which its satire is thus at a discount. The opera, incidentally, has never quite recovered from the fact that on its first production in New York seven men in succession were tried in the rôle of the Duke, and the audience saw a vastly hilarious side to the allusion that "Dukes were three a penny." The Americans called this work "The Gone-dollars."

Gilbert and Sullivan has succeeded in the United States in the main because of its music. Much of its humour is incomprehensible. In a country which is not overrun with convention, which offers no obeisance to rank, and which does not exactly elevate self-depreciation into a national habit, the satire is bound to lose its piquancy. Certainly I have never met in America many conspicuous examples of a type not unfamiliar in England. I mean :

> "The idiot who praises, with enthusiastic tone,
> All centuries but this, and every country but his own."

I have taken leave to doubt whether "The Gondoliers" is in the main a satire on snobbery. To my mind we have a better illustration of this in "Iolanthe." The Peers, as distinct from their two chief spokesmen, stand for the aloofness of their order in a supreme degree. They enter to a chorus which, in substance at least, might be a parody on the old couplet about letting trade and commerce, laws and learning, die, but leaving us still our old nobility. The opera, of course, is not so much a satire as a political extravaganza, and outside this country most of its humour is unintelligible. The Englishman appreciates it—and very heartily so—and it is more indisputably his own opera than any of its companions.

That " The Yeomen of the Guard," on the other hand, should not have transplanted successfully is astonishing. Here we have, not a satirical or a topical play, but a tender little romance which mingles laughter and tears, which never strays into the fantastic realms, which is full of fragrant melodies, and which is artistically perfect. It is true that its setting is English. It is true also that Colonel Fairfax, the swaggering soldier who is ready to meet his fate with a smile, and Jack Point, the vagabond fool who also faces his doom without whining, are typically English. And yet this seems to be a work which, above and beyond all the others of its circle, the world might have made its property. In so far as it has not done so, at least in any obvious and noticeable way, it points to one curious thing. When translated into some other language, and even when transplanted to some other soil, a virtue that we cannot define goes out of the Gilbert and Sullivan Opera.

CHAPTER V

CONTEMPTUOUS DAMAGES

GILBERT and Sullivan have been likened to the compounds of a seidlitz powder. They are effervescent only when mixed together. I think myself a more suitable simile would be that of a whisky and soda. Each, that is to say, is tolerable in itself, but the blend of stimulant and sedative is perfection. It is purely a matter of taste which ingredient should be taken in the larger quantity. But there are risks in exploring too far into such a region of alcoholic hyperbole. Let us at once get to the question. Gilbert *or* Sullivan ! Which of the two gave the greater gifts to the operas ? Is it to the dramatist or to the composer that the credit for their permanence chiefly belongs ?

Courageous is the man who would thus seek to put asunder those joined in the holy wedlock of the arts ! Gilbert *and* Sullivan is in truth an inseparable and indivisible unity. The very meddling with a conjunction has the suggestion of a heresy. Every ideal marriage is built on each partner giving of the best, and the surest road to domestic discord, it seems to me, would be for a husband and wife to argue who had been the greater contributor to the common happiness. The qualities thrown into the pool are so contrary and complementary that comparative values are impossible.

Gilbert was certainly the masculine partner. In more senses than one he was the " master " at the Savoy. He was the creative agent, the hard man of business, the business of stage-craft. The operas were a fabric of which he laid the foundation and raised the superstructure. Sullivan's was the more feminine, sensitive influence that furnished with the choicest melodic draperies the four walls, or the verbal shell, that the dramatic architect shaped. The collaboration was perfect. Why should we scheme a discord in such an age-enduring harmony ? Why should we try to make a divorce of the truest case of Darby and Joan that the English theatre has ever presented ?

Still, if Gilbert *or* Sullivan is a matter that must come to issue, the time has arrived for plain speaking. I take it that we are to differentiate them solely in their rôles as the librettist and the composer. If that is so, then surely the composer is, if not actually the greater genius, at least the partner who gives to the operas their durability and vitality. It is not so long ago that the operatic lamp was flickering. In London it went out altogether. It survived merely as a dim light in the provinces. It was the orchestral selections, played at town concerts and from pier bandstands, that kept memories fresh while a newer and baser rival, musical comedy, had temporarily edged these operas out of popularity. The Sullivanites may reasonably bring this fact to the forefront of their arguments.

Someone has said that Gilbert has been like an Old Man of the Sea around the neck of Sullivan. The inference is that his reputation is the stolen or reflected glory of the composer. Victorian dramatists who shared his contemporary fame have long since suffered eclipse. Without the aid of a melodist, who embalmed his verse in the most fragrant of tunes, all that he did would also have passed out of knowledge. Neither his wit nor his metrical astuteness has a real title to immortality. It belonged to its day; it may have been worthy of it, but by itself it would long since have followed the course of all things mortal into the twilight.

Now, to my mind, these are harsh and unfair reproaches, though they contain the half-truth that is proverbially dangerous. They suggest that Sullivan owed little to Gilbert. He owed a great deal. Sullivan had been in peril of drooping into a sentimental ecclesiastical composer, a pot-boiler of anthems and syrupy hymns, and in his early days these were " as plentiful as tabby cats, in point of fact too many." Gilbert focussed his vision on the brighter, if not precisely the higher, things. Something in his partner's muse needed " gingering up." Sullivan was a temperamental person. Some of the best of his non-theatrical music was written under the stress of deep emotional feeling. In his stage music the finest of his melodies are those wedded to the most charming and elegant lyrics. He was " a dainty man to please." He could not work at anyone's bidding. Later in his career, when other hands tried to spoon-feed him with indifferent material, he was a failure. The magic that had impelled him had gone.

It was Gilbert who gave him the impulse to write those gay and enlivening things. It was Gilbert who touched the satirical chords that were in him both as man and musician. In any case it was Gilbert who prepared all the groundwork. He it was who conceived the plots, who drew those delightful characters that people the operas, and who wrote songs so delicious in sentiment and so deft in metrical fancy. The bard went first and the minstrel followed. And yet, if there is anything eternal in these operas, it is surely the soul which the minstrel implanted. It is the music that remains as rich, as vibrating as ever in its appeal, whereas here and there the dialogue, as a few of us believe, has lost some of its sparkle. We are just taking things as we find them to-day. And the plain fact is that, while Sullivan can face the world without his Gilbert, Gilbert is a listless widower without his Sullivan.

For consider ! Sullivan's music can still stimulate the mind jaded by the cares of the day. Could it be claimed that Gilbert's humour would of itself arouse us from our lethargy ? Sullivan's music can still be heard away from its operatic setting and enchant us immensely. Could Gilbert's libretti be offered simply as spoken drama without an audience yawning ? Some dreadful moments there are in his earlier work when the verse is thin stuff in the guise of jingles and rhymes. It may be well that the music hides much of this catch-penny tinsel, clever after its own fashion, and yet given the semblance of gold by reason of the quality of the orchestral accompaniment. Stripped of the music, and clad in stark literary nakedness, it is too bad to be true.

That music should preserve its flavour longer than humour is only in the nature of things. The best joke invented could never survive repetition. A beautiful air, even if not a superlatively good one, often grows on one with each time of hearing. You can test this by the finest lyrics to be found in the operas. I would take the Merryman's Song. Here Gilbert soars into poetry. The music fits the metre adroitly, and the lilt has its own fascinations, though the composer was often more coaxing. Yet if I had to recite the words and hum the music before every meal, it would be the verse that would destroy my appetite, and in the end the repetition of it would turn me crazy.

Gilbert has been called a master of English. The best test of this is to find in his maturer works a redundant sentence or one in which the words could be more exquisitely chosen or more perfectly polished. If his writing had been slipshod, if it had been just the medium to carry the story, it might have become impossible. The type of humour is dated, shams at which he tilted have gone out of fashion or become disguised or transformed, and some of his thrusts at convention we respectfully decline to share in these less orthodox days. In a sense Sullivan's music has also become artificial. We like it in spite of the fact, and not because of the fact, that it has a simplicity that is alien to the music of this generation.

But here we reach an interesting point. Since Gilbert's time, and partly as a result of his influence, the art of the dramatist has improved. The technical standard is higher, the sense of taste is as great, the subtlety deeper. Since Sullivan's time, on the other hand, the music of the theatre has gone back, and to-day much of it is unlovely hack stuff that serves its night and perishes amidst the chills of the morning. Gilbert's successors are artists. They are his peers and he has to withstand competition. Sullivan's successors are tradesmen, turning out so many bars at so much the pound sterling, and his supremacy in theatre music these puny men have never attempted to challenge.

So far we have sought to distinguish as between the librettist and the composer. The truth is that even the two of them do not make Gilbert and Sullivan. A third element, quite as important as that of the book or the score, is the staging. Gilbert was not a dramatist only. He had not finished his work when he had delivered the script. He was an able producer endowed with a profound sense of stagecraft. And at rehearsal time his reputation was akin to that of a sergeant-major on the parade ground. He knew what he wanted, and what he wanted was law. Some of the stories told about his bluntness may be legendary, but we do know that he was a hard task-master, asking much of his principals and never suffering fools very gladly. Before the rehearsals he had pictured every detail in his mind's eye and had experimented at home with every situation on a miniature stage. He knew exactly where a principal should stand, in what manner he should act, in which way he should be funny, and how at a given moment the chorus were to be grouped. When an opera was in preparation the autocrat solicited advice from nobody—unless it were his composer. Sullivan he studied in every possible way. Letters show how anxious he was that his partner—whatever trouble it involved— should have just the right lyric.

If Gilbert had been a less masterful man, if he had not laid down the traditions of interpretation as regards the minutest points of enunciation and gesture, and if he had not commanded that these should be as unalterable as the laws of the Medes and the Persians, the operas to-day would be things of " shreds and patches." They might have been modernised, adapted and speeded up beyond recognition, and the taste and repose which commend them to us in an age of unrest would have departed. Gilbert's downright methods may sometimes have dissolved his lady artists into tears and his men into sulks and bad-tempers We need waste no sighs about them at this time of day. What we must recognise is that his apparent hardness of heart was a vital and basic contributory factor in the success of the operas.

As a coach Gilbert was without question supreme. He " made " actors and actresses out of members of his company who, while admirably equipped in many respects, were deficient in their dramatic capabilities. It meant hard work, and if sometimes he was impatient, it was because his mentality was far quicker than that of his pupils. He knew by instinct how a line should be spoken or a situation should be played. And the trouble was that a young principal could not grasp the idea for himself or convey that idea convincingly. If Gilbert had not been a dramatist, he might have become a not unsuccessful actor, though it would have been as a tragedian. He might have lacked the finished actor's restraint. During rehearsals he would show just how a thing should be done—but usually he would show it tremendously over-emphasised. If the pupil got only a third of it he would probably get as near to it as he wanted. And, meanwhile, while he was making his actors, he was insisting on refinement, naturalness and all those other qualities associated with the interpretative work at the Savoy.

So far, therefore, as we must judge as between Gilbert the dramatist and Sullivan the composer, I think we must give the verdict to Sullivan. Yet if in our fairness we are to decide what each of them brought to the operas—to the institution we know as Gilbert and Sullivan—then the scales may decline in the slightest measure in favour of Gilbert. There is not much in it really. Nor have we ever heard that the two were dissatisfied with the arrangement, or that they felt that one was giving more than his share, or less than his share, to the partnership. Like any happily married couple, they would have been scandalised that anyone should trump up a case of domestic discord against them, and they would have resented being hustled willy-nilly into the Divorce Court. My own suggestion is that no unbiassed jury would award the successful party more than contemptuous damages.

CHAPTER VI

FINDING THE REAL GILBERT

WHERE must we look for the real Gilbert ? Is he to be found in the Bab Ballads, or in the earlier non-musical plays, or in the operas ? And can we narrow down the search to any particular point ? Gilbert, one has to confess, had not an immense versatility. He toyed with variations of one idea for most of his life—the whimsicalities of fairy existence and the comicalities of topsy-turvydom. He did not do it from choice. From time to time he yearned to cut the binding strings and soar to a loftier sphere. The public would not have it, and for once the public had a surer instinct than, to be frank, a creative artist had himself as to the limits of his capabilities. Gilbert, the chronicler of topsy-turvydom, who wanted to write serious dramas, was in much the same case as the successful comedian who wants to figure as Hamlet. Neither would have succeeded.

The public, we know, has a fondness for labelling its novelists and playwrights, and it is almost resentful when they try to depart from works of a certain type, or of a certain setting, with which their names are usually coupled. In Gilbert's time there may not have been quite the same insistence on a writer getting into a groove. But the public wanted fairy plays, and it rewarded handsomely the man who could write them so inimitably. To-day the taste has changed, and the fairies have been laughed off the stage, and properly so, because these phantoms had grown tedious and silly. Yet within a year or two of Gilbert's death—and this occurred in 1911— one of his fairy plays was being given at the Savoy. It was " Fallen Fairies," a musical adaptation of an old money-making success at the Haymarket.[1] And it was one of the lamentable failures of his career. In " Iolanthe " we willingly endure a chorus of fairies, but a play chock-a-block with fairies, as this one was, was doomed from the beginning. Gilbert had been faithful to his label— but it had become time-expired a long time ago. Strange as it was, he sat down and wrote what was destined to be his last stage work, a Coliseum sketch called " The Hooligan." It was melodrama with a denouement that was harrowing and grim. Somehow, one never suspected that he could manage a " thriller " like this, and the oddest thing of all is that this gripping little work, suggesting the delirium of a murderer in the condemned cell, should prove to be the poet of fairyland's " swan-song." [2]

[1] Edward German was the composer. He did uncommonly well with impossible material. One of the defects of the play was that there were only three male characters and no mixed chorus whatever. "Fallen Fairies" was based on " The Wicked World." This play had been burlesqued under the title of " The Happy Land." Gladstone and other contemporary figures were introduced, and the play was banned, an action which later in his life the dramatist admitted was justified.

[2] " Dead—heart failure," exclaims the doctor as the curtain descends. The words, the last the dramatist wrote in his published plays, were strangely prophetic. In a short time Gilbert had died from heart failure himself.

FINDING THE REAL GILBERT

It was Gilbert's own view that the best of him went into " Broken Hearts." This explains a good deal about what we may call his innermost bias. It gives a clue to his sub-acid outlook. " Broken Hearts " is—or more properly was—a great little play. The Kendals, for whom it was written, must have had a piece to their liking. Judged by modern standards, it may be too doleful in its sentiment, and its mechanism altogether too rusty and creaky. The very idea that it should be revived in these times would shiver the box-office rafters. But to read it is a joy. It is fragrant in its tenderness and wonderful in its flow of poetical language. In superfine literary quality it might stand unchallenged. The story is that of four desolate women who,

> " Knit by the sympathy of kindred woe,
> Have sought this isle far from the ken of men :
> And having loved, and having lost our loves,
> Stand pledged to love no living thing again."

Seeing that the heart of woman must love, each of them has centred her affections on some inanimate object, and before it she keeps the idle fancy of love alive " with songs and sighs and vows of constancy." One gives her devotion to a fountain, another to a sun-dial, a third to a mirror. The Caliban-like dwarf who attends them could never make them unfaithful to their pledge. That occurs only through the arrival on the lonely island of a young and handsome prince. Two sisters fall in love with him. He speaks idle words to the younger, and when disillusionment comes, she yields her happiness to her more resolute sister and slowly pines away. It is, to be sure, a melancholy ending, but the theme is that of a rivalry of unselfishness, and it is treated in a delicate way. These are feminine women. They have forsworn the world of men, but not in the disdainful manner of those more arrogant, high-brow young ladies we meet later in "Princess Ida."

Now, if this is the real Gilbert, and if this is the play in which he most clearly expresses himself, then we are deceived by deductions about him which we draw from the operas. First and foremost he is shown to be a sentimentalist, and when elsewhere his mood is hard and brittle, we must take it that he is only pretending. He is also shown to covet the rôle of the preacher. He would sooner moralise than he would make us laugh. Above all, he loves the sweet music of words, and he prefers to wear the mantle of the poet, singing in these exquisite strains, than the merry garb of the jester. "Broken Hearts" is a serious work, and if we are to accept his plea, then his natural bent is to be a serious dramatist rather than the author of a lot of nimble tomfoolery. As a type the play belongs to fantasy. He has found his *métier*, that is to say, when he has escaped to the fanciful regions, and he likes to call to his aid, what a dramatist with two feet in the world cannot do, the supernatural and the impossible. With this one concurs without hesitation. But, as to the rest, one feels it is all the wrong hypothesis. "Broken Hearts" may have been very satisfying to him creatively. That it typified the man or the dramatist is a theory one very much questions.

If, indeed, the real Gilbert is to be found in the early plays, one would venture to suggest that he is to be discovered in "The Palace of Truth." It is certainly a coincidence that he should have been writing it when he was first introduced to Sullivan. Compared with "Broken Hearts," this is a more human play, and immeasurably a more humorous one, and the fantastic theme gives his imagination liberty. The palace is enchanted. The courtiers who visit it revel in a refreshing freedom of action and candour of tongue. For they have to learn that

> " Every one
> Who enters there is bound to speak the truth—
> The simple, unadulterated truth.
> To every question that is put to him
> He must return the unaffected truth.
> And, strange to say, while publishing the truth
> He's no idea that he is doing so."

My suggestion, and it is not a new one, is that Gilbert entered the palace of enchantment when he was young, and that he had to remain there, encircling its labyrinths and trying to find the way out, to the end of his days. It may be—and this is what he infers—that he was imprisoned unwillingly. Certainly it is true that, with all his yearning for what we call straight dramatic writing, he has vitality chiefly when he is breathing the magical atmosphere. In the kingdom of make-believe the incorrigible satirist is king. Outside his own world—the world of whimsical figures and droll situations—he never was and never would be taken at his own valuation. We may do him the justice of saying that he learnt his lesson early. He tried to desert the region of unreality, but nobody took him seriously, and he did not attempt it again. But one suspects more than once that he brooded that fate, in declining to let him do the best serious work that was in him, had treated him badly.

We come nearer to the clue to the real Gilbert when we reach " The Yeomen of the Guard." So far as he was ever autobiographical in his characters, it is in the case of Jack Point, the jester whose trial it is, even when the heart is weary and the spirit unwilling, to " quip you and crank you." Clearly, in Jack Point's story and the real-life story of his creator there is no possible parallel. But as fellow-vendors of wit they have an uncommon similarity. " I have the lighter philosophies at my tongue's tip," says Jack Point, " I can be merry, wise, quaint, grim and sardonic, one by one, or all at once." That sounds rather like Gilbert's verdict on Gilbert. Or again :

> " At prince or peer
> I aim my shaft and know no fear."

That is Gilbert certainly ! It may be Gilbert also, speaking through the mouth of the most like of all his characters, who is really lamenting that a jester must always turn a gay face to the world, even when the soul is revolting. " The public don't blame you—so long as you're funny." He had reason to know that that sardonic thrust was true. I may be stretching surmise further than it should properly go, but it is conceivable that this dramatist who wanted to be serious had himself in mind when his puppet exclaimed " for though I'm a fool," judged as a type of entertainer, " there's a limit to my folly."

One utterance of Jack Point's there is from which undeniably one may extract a good deal of meaning. Without a doubt he is Gilbert's own spokesman when he tells us that

> " When they're offered to the world in merry guise,
> Unpleasant truths are swallowed with a will—
> For he who'd make his fellow-creatures wise
> Should always gild the philosophic pill."

Here indeed is Gilbertism concentrated and complete ! It is the Gilbert gospel enunciated to a nicety. You will notice that it discards the idea that a humorist's aim should be humour simply and solely. The jester aches to wear a surplice over the motley. In different words he admitted it in his autobiography. So that the homilies may be more easily swallowed, and so that this childish world may be deluded for its own good, he adds a little jam to each spoonful. The home truths do thus seem a little less acid ; but did this author really, really believe that anyone ever cared a toss for his precepts, whether administered plain or disguised ? The odd thing is that apparently he meant that the sugar was of lesser account than the pill. We had the comedy merely so that we could assimilate the philosophy. It has been stupid of us to think that it was exactly the opposite.

I fancy that the real Gilbert is to be found in the Bab Ballads. They were mostly the work of his immaturity, but they were the work also of the time when his outlook was fresher, when his heart should have been eager and joyous, and when whatever was in him welled up spontaneously and unaffectedly. Before fame came to him, and before he was beset with prejudices and predilections, he could write just as he felt, and his public was still in the making. And in one of these happy verses he inscribes what might be his own dedication.[1] It is the confession that, freely and of his own accord, he had entered the enchanted palace, the happy kingdom of make-believe and paradox. It was the dream of the man who thought

> " That somewhere he had come
> To dwell in Topsy-Turvydom,
> Where vice is virtue, virtue vice,
> Where nice is nasty, nasty nice,
> Where right is wrong, and wrong is right,
> Where white is black, and black is white."

In other words, he was going to turn things upside-down, and many of the conventions and a

[1] See article by Dr. J. M. Bulloch, *Gilbert and Sullivan Journal*, February 1925.

few of the verities would soon have to show whether or not they were shock-proof. The Gilbert of the Bab Ballads tilted at windmills for the very fun of the thing. The Gilbert of the operas tilted at them with just a touch of pedantry.

Really, the most topsy-turvy thing Gilbert ever wrote was an early effort, rarely remembered to-day, called " Topsy-Turvydom." It carries his favourite theme to its uttermost limits. So complete has been the somersault that " children are born learned, and they gradually forget everything until, as old men, they are utterly ignorant." [1] Vice is rewarded and virtue punished. Cowards are honoured and brave men elbowed aside. Honest men are arrested by thieves. The Prime Minister, a very popular man, enters with a top and hoop. He is received with hoots and groans, the topsy-turvy method of expressing applause, and it is explained that his unfitness is the one and sufficient qualification for his position. This is indeed Gilbertism at its very pinnacle ! And it was presented exactly a year before the production—though probably not before the actual writing—of " Trial by Jury."

I have not seen the text of this extravaganza, but it might help to confirm one's suspicions that, although it was written at a time when the dramatist was no longer a novice, he was tackling a subject too big for his powers. Certainly it was not a

[1] This is an extract from Gilbert's note-book, and the entry is quoted fully in Dark and Grey's *W. S. Gilbert : His Life and Letters.* The statement in that book that it was written " some years before his death " should surely read " forty years before his death."

success. It was produced at the opening of the Criterion Theatre in 1874, and on referring back to a leading newspaper's criticism, I was interested to discover that the reference to it occupied less than ten lines, though the better part of a column is devoted to the criticism of the companion play, H. J. Byron's " An American Lady." In the critic's view, this piece, though richly equipped in the way of dresses and decoration, had a humour too subtle to be perceived immediately by even an exceptionally intelligent audience, though it had an undeniable ingenuity in bringing into employment the talents of the performers.[1] The only answer to this is that the humour was subtle only in the sense that it was in advance of its day. After five weeks the piece was removed from the programme.

Going back, however, to the matter of Gilbert's serious efforts, it is a fact that when he reached fame he never tried to thrust serious work on the public. Necessity did not require it of him—and possibly it was just as well for his reputation. " Pygmalion and Galatea," " Broken Hearts " and " Gretchen " have some claims to survive as literature, though two of them were failures on the stage. We may have doubts whether, with all his gifts and sense of stage-craft, his was the calibre that can produce a dramatic masterpiece. In the making of a modern masterpiece, as we shall urge later, he might have been hopeless. The serious plays which he wrote in his earlier days rarely stormed the ramparts of

---

[1] The newspaper was the *Daily Telegraph*.

public approval. That fact is said to have made him resentful. The reason, after all, may not have been exclusively that he thought he was getting less than his merits, but rather the feeling that, when he went in with his own bat, he did not make much of an innings. To a man who, like himself, was not surfeited with modesty, this may have been galling.

CHAPTER VII

TAKING GILBERT'S MEASURE

IT is curious that Gilbert, incomparably the most gifted humorous writer of his day, never impresses us as being himself an essentially humorous person. He was not the kind of man who, having thought out a delicious witticism, would chuckle heartily as he put it on paper. He was not the kind of man who would throw his cap into the air on any pretext. Outward enthusiasm he regarded as a trifle vulgarian. No doubt when he wrote a good line his artistic soul would be satisfied, but one fancies that this indulgence would never rise beyond, in Nanki-Poo's words, the limits of " modified rapture."

That he was a lover of life one has no wish to question. That he had the real *joie de vivre*, that his impulses were ever really spontaneous and hearty, are matters on which the evidence is unconvincing. There was that sardonic strain in his make-up. It shows itself even in the best of his humour. Sullivan's music softens the asperities of it again and again. The point in the more authentic of those innumerable anecdotes told about him is almost invariably biting. The happier jests which

68

he is said to have made in the social circle rarely deserve preservation. You could accuse this master of humour of lacking a sense of humour, and you would be, of course, woefully wrong. But at the same time you would come uncommonly near to touching the spot.

Gilbert, the master of paradox, was a paradox in his own person. We should have expected the inventor of these merry situations to relish life itself with a roguish heart and a slyly mischievous eye. We know that in real life he was masterful and inclined to be gruff. We are told that he hated enthusiasms and had a dislike of reforms. It seems altogether probable. Yet this hater of enthusiasms was the mainspring of one enthusiasm that has become a public fetish and an obsession. I refer to the flood-tide of enthusiasm, never more active than now, that swells at the mention of Gilbert and Sullivan. The people to whom the operas are an ecstasy, and who will not endure one breath of criticism about them, are legion.

This man who disliked reforms was also one of the great reformers of his own generation. By his influence the English stage was drawn out of the mire of banality and unwholesomeness and lifted artistically to a much higher plane. In his plays he mocks at social conventions and turns things topsy-turvy. In real life he was as conventional and as matter-of-fact as a good suburban grocer. He allows his characters to revel in an orgy of happy-go-lucky inconsequence. Yet in his own business, that of presenting a play, he would no more endure slip-shod methods, either in himself or in others, than he would strut like an aesthetic along Piccadilly. Long before the phrase had been turned into a slogan, he was a believer in, and a ruthless practitioner of, the gospel of " one hundred per cent. efficiency."

It was because he was efficient, and because he was in a position to require more than lip service to efficiency, that the operas remain so enchanting. Gilbert, after all, was a lucky man, a very lucky man, in many respects. He had the luck to arrive just when the theatre was ready to be stirred out of its ineptitude. He had the luck to find in Sullivan an ideal collaborator for the ingenious line of fancy he was exploiting. He had the luck to find in Grossmith a type of comedian to whom he could model his own conceptions of comedy parts. He had the luck to find in D'Oyly Carte a manager who was a genius in organisation and foresight. He had the luck many times to be the fortunate child of happy accident.[1] He had the luck, above all, to be installed as a dictator who could insist on every detail that his artistic mind had planned, and who need make no little concessions here and

[1] Two facts connected with *The Mikado* will serve to illustrate this point. Gilbert determined at rehearsals to cut out " My object all sublime." It was only in answer to earnest entreaty that he spared this capital song. At the first night Grossmith stumbled when singing " The Flowers that bloom in the Spring." It was quite an unrehearsed incident, but to the audience it was immensely diverting, and ever since Ko-Ko has had to stumble and maintain a comic sitting position until the end of the song.

there to satisfy nincompoops of crude judgment. Such a combination of luck, even when allied with natural gift, as it certainly was, would be the envy of any modern playwright. If he had not been a dictator, neither the merriment nor the melodies of these operas, or even the two combined, could have given them their time-resisting qualities.

I am leading up to a nice speculation. If Gilbert had been content with lesser standards, and if his nature had been softer, would his story have been written rather differently? I repeat that it is a nice speculation. Little as I like to use the word, I think he had certain constitutional defects which are found, though only on a close analysis, to have reflected themselves in the plays. The characters, taking them all in all, are righteous and orderly people. In manners they can be almost insufferably perfect. They are as Victorian as the Victorian who created them. They are not a passionate lot. They are never intense about anything, they have no burning enthusiasms, and their snobbery towards the lower orders is simply profound. They offer few thoughts that would help this weary world in solving its problems. They may help it to forget its cares for the while, but that is an irrelevant point, and it only re-affirms their artificiality. Gilbert was far, far from being insincere or artificial himself, but in most other respects his stage children pay their tribute to heredity.

An able critic has said that Gilbert's world is " remote from life." So, he insists, are his characters.[1] But in those times nearness to life on the stage was not expected. Wagner's world is more remote still, though he belonged to a nation that has a bent towards the mythological, and grand opera habitually divorces itself from reality. The point has greater force at a time when we see a certain dramatic school getting so close up to life that even some of the sanctities are no longer respected. Gilbert's figures are not so remote that we cannot take them as types. Shabby gentility still masquerades itself at times under a twopenny pageantry. The pluralist continues to function. The political placeman does his loyal hack-work and gets his promotion. They are not called the Duke of Plaza-Toro, Pooh-Bah or Sir Joseph Porter, but they are second cousins to those worthies, and the family resemblance is plain. And there are others.

But we come at last to the question whether Gilbert, had he lived in a later age, would have been a peer amongst his brother dramatists, or just an underling. I know it is a futile matter to argue what any man might do were he re-born in a new generation. Gilbert wrote for his day—with his collaborator he wrote for longer than that—and he was necessarily bound to conditions and limitations which were prevailing. But at the same time one doubts whether his endowments were the endowments asked for by the present-day stage.

---

[1] H. M. Walbrook in *Gilbert and Sullivan Opera.*

He was no intellectual.[1]   He never could be profound.   George Bernard Shaw is a far better
thinker—and we have to put up with his preaching.
Gilbert was curiously detached from the actualities
of life, and he had not that keen sympathy, judged
by his plays, that would ever cause him to ride
about redressing human wrongs.   He was no " hot
gospeller " aflame with a message.[2]   He could
flick at a foible, but he could not thunder at an
injustice, partly because comic opera is not a good
medium for thunder, but chiefly because he was
not built that way.   Galsworthy, who comes so
much nearer to the hard and harsh facts of life,
would beat him out of the field.   He might be a
rival to Barrie.   They both have a taste for soaring
into the realms of fantasy.   But the real Barrie
never loses contact with the earth for long.   He
has, further, a more subtle humour, and he is
probably at his best when he discards the cap and
bells altogether, which is something the older hand
was wise enough for his own sake rarely to try.

Gilbert was a humorist—a man whose one job
it was to make us laugh.   It is useless to say he did
or could do anything higher.   But as a humorist he
was one in a thousand.   Compare him with the
common crowd of witty writers, and he stands out

[1] Gilbert's development as a dramatist is ably discussed by Dr. T.
Stephenson, *Gilbert and Sullivan Journal*, April 1926.

[2] *Charity* was his one so-called problem play.   It held up to con-
demnation the harsh moral judgments of its day towards a woman in
whose life there had been a lapse.   It ran only eight nights.   The
public called it immoral !

73

supremely by reason of that unusual combination of his ingenious fancy, his gift of making humour always wholesome and tasteful, his splendid stage technique, and his choiceness of style. He stood alone in his time for one other reason. The Victorians did not want to be bothered with problems. The social conscience was still undeveloped. The gospel of *laissez faire* was an unwritten law. They wanted nothing but the rigidly conventional in their novels and on the stage. The earlier dramatists were not the sort who could take them out of the rut. Gilbert himself did not shake them out of their complacency. But he did give their complacency a jolt. Life, which to them was so sedate and orderly, was pictured invertedly. Customs which were as settled as the rising and the setting of the sun were turned topsy-turvy. A Victorian daughter who had marched into the boudoir with an Eton crop and a cigarette would have been an apparition no more staggering.

It has been argued that a good deal of humour amuses people because it shocks them.[1] It may be because our morals are shocked that we are ready to reward the daring of certain modern playwrights. Gilbert's shocks, of course, were never of that unwholesome order, but they must have been shocks nevertheless to a staid and convention-clogged age. To-day, it has been said, we are accustomed to the unexpected, and we feel no

[1] This theory is one advanced by Clifford Bax in an interesting letter in *The Spectator*.

violence when it is suggested that, after all, life is not an orderly thing. In that respect we have grown shock-proof. We are not unwilling to be shocked in some other way. The Victorians must have felt more pleasantly shocked than we do by the vision of a world turned topsy-turvy. Gilbert's fanciful world was in such curious contrast to their own life and ideas. And the chaste Victorian leg was subjected to a good deal of pulling.

CHAPTER VIII

GUSTS OF COMMON SENSE

You will remember the strange denouement in
"Ruddigore." It was the fate of the bad baronets
that they must commit a crime daily. Failure to
commit it meant death. The reward of success
was almost as grim. They had to live on and on
until they sickened of the iniquity of their existence
and automatically perished. It was only by re-
fusing to do their daily crime that they could find
the way to the grave. Upon all this Robin indulges
in some very close reasoning. He points out that
a baronet's refusal to commit his crime is tanta-
mount to suicide. But suicide is in itself a crime,
and the baronet who commits suicide, therefore,
has done his duty and ought not to be dead ! If
you can grasp these subtleties you must agree that
they are irresistibly logical. Sir Roderic, who is
re-visiting the ancestral castle as a ghost, finds it
so convincing that, *ipso facto*, he returns to life on
the spot. He not only returns to life, but he
marries a faithful old sweetheart, a charming sequel
to the years of ghost-hood.

Gilbert has a knack of finishing his operas in
this kind of way. I do not mean, of course, that

he usually brings the dead to life and hurries them off to the altar, a departure which we whose habit it is to put marriage earlier in our scheme of things might find a trifle disturbing. I am referring to his method of drowning absurdities in a last cold douche of logic. They are absurdities which he himself has contrived, but they have to be got rid of before the curtain comes down, and this he does on an almost invariable plan. He either laughs them out of court frankly or he inflates them into such super-absurdities that they collapse under their own very weight. Laboriously the house of cards has been built up, but in the end there comes one lusty gust of common sense, and the flimsy edifice crumbles. It may be comic common sense—it usually is—but even this is useful in solving a tangle.

" Iolanthe " is not, perhaps, the best illustration of these methods, but it will serve the purpose. It seems that affairs have reached a state of deadlock. Every fairy who marries a mortal must die. That is the law of Fairyland. Yet the Fairies have married the Peers—oh ! what a delicious idea ! —and strict adherence to the law would mean their wholesale slaughter. Even the stern-minded Queen finds the prospect appalling. Here it is that the Lord Chancellor shows that " the subtleties of the legal mind are equal to the emergency." A single alteration will put matters right. Let the law read that every fairy who does *not* marry a mortal shall die—and the difficulty is solved immediately. Seemingly the Queen had never thought of this, but without more ado she pencils in the amendment, an awkward constitutional dilemma is solved, and she herself prepares under this new code to become Mrs. Willis. And we and these blissful couples soon resume our journeys rejoicing.

In " Iolanthe " one might suspect—and it was probably true—that Gilbert was a hard-crusted Tory. A few personal predilections seem to peep out through his puppets. But before one can pin him down to the party he claims to belong to he has slipped off at a tangent. In " The Gondoliers," on the other hand, he is caught sketching a plausible case for a Socialistic State, that so-called " Monarchy re-modelled on Republican principles." Our Baratarian theorists do not reduce mankind to one common level. They raise mankind upwards. They have the gospel of brotherhood carried to its ultimate and most beneficent limits. Seeing that a cook is as good as a king, and if anything better, there is no reason why his little vanities should not be suitably flattered, and why he should not be adorned by gorgeous raiment and a title worthy of his Lord High Cookship. It makes life so much sweeter when a hardy son of toil can bask in the splendours of a courtly flummery. Here, indeed, is the golden age when majesty itself takes a turn in the sentry-box, not as an act of gracious condescension, but as a gesture demanded of equality.

The thing is so absurd that it breaks down under its own weight. It is the Socialistic idea in full blast, though possibly a little more colourful and elegant, and certainly a little more zestful, than its real-life visionaries ever imagine. The dream will not work. Gilbert smashes it with a phrase. "When all are promoted to the top of the tree, then everyone is somebodee, and no one's anybody"! The Grand Inquisitor, an individualist if ever there was one, could not have put the case for individualism more precisely.

"Utopia" is Gilbert's cleverest satire and his most complete essay into paradox. England and its institutions are held up as a model by the simple Utopians. Actually the play is a shrewd tilt at many things which are, or which are alleged to be, typically English. He has been accused of writing it from the angle of a jaundiced foreigner. That I think is absurd. He wrote as an Englishman who, with all her faults, could love his country still, and who could indulge in levities which are never taken amiss by any sane and healthy fellow-Englishman. My point at the moment is the " sting in the tail " of " Utopia." So complete has been the reformation that the doctors are starving, the lawyers' occupation has gone, the prisons are empty, and war has become impossible. Idealism has defeated itself. The Utopian dream breaks down, as it is bound to break down in any active, work-a-day society. That is the logic of the thing. By changing all this, these disillusioned people discover, there will be "sickness in plenty, endless lawsuits, crowded jails, interminable confusion in the Army and Navy, and, in short, general and unexampled prosperity." The means whereby the revival is to be brought about is the introduction of party government. That, of course, is a bluff bit of humour, but the house of cards has been toppled over already.

In " Princess Ida " a comic platitude knocks the bottom out of a good deal of fantastic theory. Near the end there is a perilous prospect that the Princess will remain a blue stocking in Castle Adamant. And that would offend the sacred principle that in no circumstances must a stage heroine be left to linger on as a spinster (or in this case as a grass widow). She foresees, this ultra-feminist before her time, that posterity may yet bow down to her exalted name in gratitude. " But if," asks Hildebrand, " you enlist all women in your cause, and make them all abjure tyrannic man, how is this posterity to be provided ? " Truly, as a listener comments later, this opens " an unbounded field for speculation." Princess Ida is the kind of didactic young lady who would ordinarily argue the hind leg off a donkey. But, the hour growing late, this poser is allowed to leave her nonplussed. " I never thought of that," is her naïve reply. And in a few moments Ida, the contrite man-hater, renews her vows to the man to whom she was married when a twelve months' old baby. It comes as a swift climax. Most of Gilbert's climaxes come pretty swiftly.

" Patience " is a gust of common sense all the

way through. It is ridicule in the form of the ridiculous. The play was written when the aesthetic craze was the fashion, and sheer satire could do its part without the aid of fantasy, contradictions, or paradox. Here is another instance where the method of attack is that of transforming an absurdity into a super-absurdity. The real aesthetics were never really as crazy as they were painted. Yet, to put it at the least, they were unconventional and they were un-English. In real life Gilbert was conventional and matter-of-fact to a degree. In the theatre he was supremely the opposite. He was face to face with a cult which, as a man, he must have found offensive, but which as a satirist must have appealed to him irresistibly. When "Patience" was produced aestheticism had passed its zenith already. The opera certainly gave it the last kick into the grave.

But here let me add a foot-note about "Patience." I repeat that the aesthetic craze was not really as bad as it has been painted. In essence it was a revolt against the drabness and the materialism of contemporary life, and it sought to introduce a little colour, possibly a little mental freshness, into a stodgy and a dowdy atmosphere. Not all its disciples were poseurs. Like other movements, it became ridiculous through the excesses of its extremists, who made aestheticism an excuse for vainglory and flamboyancy, which actually are its opposites. The better influences of the movement bore fruit in a later day.

Now, Gilbert had a hatred of shams, and it is not unnatural that he should have wanted to scourge the picturesque zealots who thrust their vanities into the limelight. But he was also a lover of beauty. He could not have been against the movement in its broader and worthier aspect. I have rather a suspicion that for once, and against his better judgment, he was trimming his sails to the favouring breezes. The very idea of aestheticism must have been odious to those stuffy people who wanted nothing more than to be left to wallow in their stodginess. They were sure to acclaim him, and they would have been the first to be scandalised had he put his curates on to the stage, as his intention had been when he began writing the opera. As a concession to the dull respectability of the time it was not very heroic.

CHAPTER IX

SATIRE AND LOGIC

SATIRE, in its literary aspect, has been defined as an expression in adequate terms of the sense of amusement or disgust exhibited by the ridiculous or the unseemly, providing that humour is a distinctly recognisable element, and that the utterance is invested with literary form. Without humour satire is invective and without literary form it is mere clownish jeering.[1]

Gilbert without a doubt satisfies the conditions of this definition. The humour of his satire and its literary form are certainly recognisable qualities. I fancy that his only lapse into invective is to be found in one of Robin Oakapple's songs in "Ruddigore." In most of his satire there is a curious blend of pointedness and pleasantry. The arrow hits but does not hurt. It loses its venom, so far as it ever has any, at the moment of impact.

A feature of Gilbert's humour is that it is dignified. It is "common" neither in its conception nor in its literary presentation. It is not only that the humour

---

[1] This paragraph is a textual quotation from an article on Satire in the *Encyclopædia Britannica*.

is seemly. The diction itself, while it may not be eloquent, is most certainly elegant. It has choiceness, smoothness, and polish. You may read his libretti with the sense that you are reading literature and his lyrics with the sense that you are reading poetry. The merit, it is true, is not always equal, but the standard is immeasurably higher than that of the stage writers at the time he began.

And much of Gilbert's humour is verbal humour. By this I mean that the essence of it is, not alone the humour of ideas, but the play upon words, the adroit turning of rhymes, the quiet irony that is given to trifling and colloquial phrases. Many of his witty ideas become wittier still because of the quaintness of their literary shape. He can contrive amusing situations and he can draw interesting figures. But often there is the suggestion that these are just the backgrounds for the display of his verbal ingenuity. You will notice that most of his chief characters, whatever their oddities may be, have an uncommon gift for neat, fanciful phrases.

At times Gilbert's style inclines towards the " Johnsonesque." He loves the sonorous big word, not for its own sake, but for the sake, I think, of " effect." It enforces the note of affectation and pomposity that is struck in some of the plays. At other times there is no writer more simple or precise. He wrote very quickly, but then came the work of revision, the pruning of superfluous words, the search for the deft shades of meaning, the patient literary polishing. Sometimes he would rewrite a libretto a dozen times before he was satisfied. We are told that Robin Oakapple's address to the ancestral pictures originally consisted of three pages of closely written manuscript.[1] Gilbert condensed and condensed until there was not a word that did not serve its purpose. He took three months in perfecting that speech. It is now only sixty words long, beginning with " Oh ! my forefathers," and ending with " Let the sweet psalm of that repentant hour soften your long-dead hearts, and tune your souls to mercy on your poor posterity."

Let us return to the question of his use, as a deliberate aid to comic effect, of rotund phraseology. We have one illustration of it in the case of Ralph Rackstraw. Says this common seaman :

" In me there meet a combination of antithetical elements which are at eternal war with one another. Driven hither by objective influences—thither by subjective emotions —wafted one moment into the blazing day by mocking hope—plunged the next into the Cimmerian darkness of tangible despair, I am but a living ganglion of irreconcilable antagonisms."

This is not at all bad from the lips of a man who apologises soon afterwards for his lack of education and polité accomplishments. So far there has been no evidence that Ralph Rackstraw knows that he is a man of good birth, and if he does know it, then he is a poor hand at disguise. Pooh-Bah, who is more likely to have a massive vocabulary, speaks of

[1] See Henry A. Lytton's *Secrets of a Savoyard*.

" merely corroborative detail intended to give artistic verisimilitude to a bald and unconvincing narrative." In "Patience" the aesthetics talk about an "aesthetic transfiguration," the "transcendentality of delirium," and the "earnestly precious." Even the Duke of Dunstable, a very ordinary person, asks in the same opera whether he is "particularly intelligent, or remarkably studious, or excruciatingly witty, or unusually accomplished, or exceptionally virtuous." The sentence certainly makes no point of crispness.

In most of these instances the elaborate words have been used for "effect." It is in the songs, and particularly the patter songs, that Gilbert of his own free will, if one may put it that way, indulges a taste for (forgive my own modest imitation of it !) syllabic prolixity. He does so in order that he can give scope to his rhythmical agility. And the manner in which he can string together big words, in lines that scan well and never falter for a dexterous rhyme, is clever to a degree. Major-General Stanley, who is not an ornate phrase-maker as a rule, proclaims :

" I know the kings of England, and I quote the fights historical ;
From Marathon to Waterloo, in order categorical ;
I'm very well acquainted, too, with matters mathematical,
I understand equations, both the simple and quadratical,
About binomial theorem I'm teeming with a lot o' news.
With many cheerful facts about the square on the hypotenuse."

—a good example of the dexterity of the patter song, and one in which the dramatist's skill in verbal athletics is more deliberately exploited than it is, for instance, in Colonel Calverley's song of the Heavy Dragoon. Here there is a play on sonorous words, but the greater feat is, perhaps, the nimbleness and sureness with which difficult allusions succeed one another in a sweeping procession :

" If you want a receipt for this soldier-like paragon,
  Get at the wealth of the Czar (if you can),
The family pride of a Spaniard from Arragon,
  Force of Mephisto pronouncing a ban,
A smack of Lord Waterford, reckless and rollicky,
  Swagger of Roderick, heading his clan,
The keen penetration of Paddington Pollaky,
  Grace of an Odalisque on a divan,
The genius strategic of Caesar on Hannibal,
Skill of Sir Garnet in thrashing a cannibal,
Flavour of Hamlet, the Stranger—a touch of him,
Little of Manfred (but not very much of him),
  Beadle of Burlington, Richardson's show,
  Mr. Micawber and Madame Tussaud !
    Take of these elements all that is fusible,
    Melt them all down in a pipkin or crucible,
    Set them to simmer and take off the scum,
    And a Heavy Dragoon is the residuum ! "

I make two more poetical quotations—two from a very large number—to illustrate this side of my subject. The first is a simpler verse, very neat in form, and metrically ingenious. It occurs in the chorus of the Bucks and Blades in " Ruddigore " :

GILBERT AND SULLIVAN

> " From charms intramural
>> To prettiness rural
>> The sudden transition
>> Is simply Elysian,
>> So come, Amaryllis,
>> Come, Chloe and Phyllis,
> Your slaves, for the moment, are we ! "

And the other is an extract from Ludwig's song in " The Grand Duke." Here, once more, there is a taste for juggling with sonorous words, this time even with a classic smattering :

> " We've a choir hyporchematic (that is, ballet-operatic)
>> Who respond to the *choreutæ* of that cultivated age,
> And our clever chorus-master, all but captious criticaster
>> Would accept as the *choregus* of the early Attic stage
> This return to classic ages is considered in their wages,
>> Which are always calculated by the day or by the week,
> And I'll pay 'em (if they'll back me) all in *oboloi* and *drachmæ*
>> Which they'll get (if they prefer it) at the Kalends that
>> are Greek."

" Gilbertism " has been held to be a term descriptive of a conflict between the well-balanced mind of a serious man and the exuberant spirit of his impish counterpart.[1] This is a shrewd definition. Gilbert, indeed, does not give us a contrast between sense and nonsense, but rather that between sense and inconsequence. It is the imp of mischief that merrily flits through these operas and topples so many of our accepted notions topsy-turvy. The so-called serious mind sees the obvious from a new and comical angle. It may be convention, it may

---

[1] Edith A. Browne in *W. S. Gilbert*.

be mannerism, it may be logic. But, whichever it is, the imp gives it a twist and tilts it out of the ordinary. Because it is inconsequence—and not sheer nonsense—we are never very far away from reality. We can see that it is with the things of our own world that the sprite has been playing.

Convention is Gilbert's chief satirical target. He attacks it again and again, but he usually ends by implying that, taken on the whole, convention is not a bad thing. He satirises caste, and he introduces us to an upside-down world in which love is supposed to level rank, to turn peers into pirates, and to transform gondoliers into kings. This is the delightful make-believe of the impish counterpart. Before it is over the serious man takes control and shows that these visions are crazy and impossible. The one exception to this occurs in " Iolanthe." The characters do not come down to earth, as their habit is in most of the operas, but soar away " up in the sky ever so high." For once the spirit of fantasy is allowed to reign all the way through.

At times the imp attempts to be more logical than the logical. It sounds logical that all men should be equal. It sounds logical that the punishment should fit the crime. It sounds logical that a primitive land, by borrowing the clothes and the customs of civilisation, and by applying its laws and its commercial ethics, should become as prosperous as a civilised country. In three of the plays these ideas are put into practice. Everything seems to be going well until a few gusts of common sense expose the flaws in the logic. It is shown to be a fallible instrument, too theoretical to be workable, and things are better left as they are.

Gilbert's verbal humour, as I have called it, also makes play with logic. The moral of it is that, if only you carry it far enough, you can make logic prove anything. By following a specious line of argument, and with no questions asked, it is possible to demonstrate that black is white, and right is wrong. It is Gilbert's favourite way of giving the impish counterpart notice to quit and putting an end to the operas. In the preceding chapter I have shown how he contrives the curtain for " Iolanthe," for " Princess Ida," and (better still) for " Ruddigore." In much the same fashion Ko-Ko is able in the end to mollify the benevolent autocrat in " The Mikado " :

" When your Majesty says ' Let a thing be done ' it's as good as done—practically it *is* done—because your Majesty's will is law. Your Majesty says ' Kill a gentleman,' and a gentleman is told off to be killed. Consequently, that gentleman is as good as dead—practically he *is* dead—and if he is dead why not say so ? "

—and Lady Angela gives an apparently conclusive reason why the rapturous maidens should have renounced their aestheticism in " Patience " :

" Archibald the All-Right cannot be all-wrong, and if the All-Right chooses to discard aestheticism, it proves that aestheticism ought to be discarded."

In the former case the Mikado's reply is that

90

"nothing could possibly be more satisfactory." Perhaps *we* had better leave it at that.

Logic—or a perverted excess of it—involves some of the characters in mental entanglements. We may note two examples of many. There is the case of the Lord Chancellor when he considers the dilemma of a man in his office who is in love with a ward of his court. Can he, asks this debater of knotty problems, give his own consent to his own marriage to his own ward? Can he marry her without his consent? Can he, if he marries her, be committed for contempt of his own court, and can he appear by counsel before himself to move an arrest of his own judgment? Such are the conflicts of mind of a man who would carry deduction to its logical extremity. Pooh-Bah also finds himself in a logical cleft-stick. You remember that remarkably well-written passage in which he discusses the question of making a suitable State appropriation for Ko-Ko's marriage :

"Of course, as First Lord of the Treasury, I could propose a special vote that would cover all expenses, if it were not that, as leader of the Opposition, it would be my duty to resist it tooth and nail. Or, as Paymaster-General, I could so cook the accounts that, as Lord High Auditor, I should never discover the fraud. But then, as Archbishop of Titipu, it would be my duty to denounce my dishonesty and give myself into my own custody as First Commissioner of Police."

Such are the troubles, not of a master pluralist, but of a logician who sees things rather too clearly.

Now and then Gilbert uses humour—to quote one of his characters—to " gild the philosophic pill." A good deal of philosophy of sorts is to be found in the operas. It rarely has originality and it never has depth. What it does do is to enshrine a few wise maxims in acceptable phrases. Gilbert's philosophy—and there could be none better—is that of seeing the bright side and living life with a zest. " For, look you," says honest Jack Point " there is humour in all things, and the truest philosophy is that which teaches us to find it and to make the most of it." A very wise saying ! It is the basis of all that is good in Gilbert and Sullivan Opera.

CHAPTER X

SULLIVAN THE HUMORIST

GILBERTISM was the invention of—Gilbert. And the first convert to Gilbertism that its creator made was—Sullivan. So far as Gilbertian humour could have a musical counterpart, the composer was able to embody it, though the parallel was not complete. Gilbertism is in essence topsy-turvydom. Now, whatever Sullivan was or was not, he was an orderly craftsman, choosing his melodic patterns and dressing his themes with the nicety of a dude before the looking-glass. He also—and this is more to the immediate point—looked on life from an ordinary angle. Gilbert, to be sure, was as orderly and as rational in his normal outlook as most men, but he did rather stand on his head before writing a play. This was not the case with Sullivan. He did not find musical ideas and treat them invertedly. There is nothing whatever in his music that relates it to the topsy-turvy sphere. But, this distinction having been made, one may say that he is as witty musically as his partner is witty. He is as adroit, as nimble and as resourceful as his partner is all these things dramatically, and his idioms are possibly even more smooth and polished than his partner's literary

93

idioms are smooth and polished. For the moment I want to stress his claims as a witty composer.

Sullivan's score has humorous touches in plenty. Let me remind you of a few only. Take " The Mikado." If the bassoon, that licensed comedian of instruments, does not laugh right out when the three little maids are telling their story, how else can one describe it, please ? Listen at Ko-Ko's reference to the criminal's shriek to the manner in which the oboe takes a hand in a game. Listen, again, to Pitti-Sing's declaration that the criminal whistled an air, did he, and hear how the flute gives a roguish point to the saying. In " Iolanthe " the pizzicato notes that introduce the fairies always seem to me a satirical jest. The fairies are not real fairies at all, but so many young ladies tripping in on not too elfin-like toes, a pretty bit of pretence. Sullivan's introduction for real fairies would surely have been more gossamer. In " H.M.S. Pinafore " the swish of the nautical buckets is comically conveyed in the line about " the tar who ploughs the water." Captain Corcoran's breezy song of a model commander and a model crew is introduced by a recitative that might have been taken bodily from " The Messiah." In its way it is a capital joke. Then in " Iolanthe " there is Private Willis's song, and those three notes at the end, so expressive of the sentry's boredom with the ordinariness of politics. And where may you find a drier bit of musical humour than the few notes that illustrate that droll fancy in " Ruddigore " :

SULLIVAN THE HUMORIST

" Cheerily carols the lark
Over the cot.
Merrily whistles the clerk
Scratching a blot " ?

In " The Gondoliers " a medley of traditional airs is worked into the accompaniment to Don Alhambra's " There lived a King." Listen to it, and you will hear snatches of the British National Anthem and " Rule, Britannia," a few bars of a hornpipe to illustrate the line " with admirals the ocean teemed," and the waggish introduction of a Scottish reel to point the reference to " toddy." In the same ironic fashion the air of " Rule, Britannia " serves as the prelude to the finale of " Utopia."

" Princess Ida " has one of the big musical jokes in the operas. It is that trio for Gama's warrior sons, written in the best Handel manner, and it indicates that Sullivan could write that kind of jog-trot stuff if he wanted. A clever burlesque of the florid Italian style occurs in the double chorus in " The Pirates of Penzance." Equally mock-heroic in strain is the entrance of the Dragoons in " Patience." It is a bustling tune, quite good after a fashion, and yet suggesting that, if the stereotyped methods of writing a military march were called for, this composer could turn it out as readily as anyone. Sullivan, in fact, had a rare sense of humour, both actually and musically. Some of the mad rhymes which his colleague gave him could be tackled only with a merry heart and a twinkling eye. An over-serious composer would have been baffled completely. Sullivan could master them; he could give a merry lilt to the happiest and the oddest of lyrics, and he could slip in a sly dig on his own account at the conventionalities of his musical brethren, contemporary or past.

It was said of Gluck, with what truth we need not consider, that he put the statue in the orchestra and placed the pedestal on the stage. This was never Sullivan's fault. He is always kind to his singers. He knew, none better, how to write for the voice, and he knew what was due to it in combination with other instruments. Barrington once coined a happy metaphor. It was that Sullivan's accompaniment was a lifeboat to the singer instead of a foaming wave to submerge him. And that is true. Sullivan's accompaniments are often delightfully descriptive and playful, but they are never in the least obtrusive, and never do they seek to attract interest away from the stage. The spotlight, as it were, has to be focussed, not on the orchestra, but on the singer. As instances of this we have the rippling accompaniment that adorns Major-General Stanley's " Softly sighs the river," though it is never made more than a subsidiary feature, and the picturesque musical comment which accompanies the Lord Chancellor's " When you're lying awake." And of this consideration for the singer there are evidences throughout the operas. Many of the accompaniments seem to me to suggest nothing so much as a man chuckling over his own joke, but with his hand before his mouth, lest he should be impolite or disturbing to someone who is speaking (or singing).

For several reasons it is well to remember the musical environment in which the composer grew up. He was one of the children of the Chapel Royal. It was this ecclesiastical environment and his experiences as a choir-boy that gave him an unrivalled grounding in vocal and choral technique. But the atmosphere of it was terribly stuffy. Sir Richard Terry has properly said that in Sullivan's early days music was under the " benumbing influence of the organ loft." [1] Handel oratorio, mangled out to the same old pattern, held music generally in a creeping paralysis. Spohr, Mendelssohn and Sterndale-Bennett had carried on the tradition, and the lesser lights were following suit with the dull obedience of commonplace minds. It was laboured music, mostly in oratorio or cantata form, and written first and foremost from the angle of organ technique.

Such was the enervating musical air that he breathed during his youth. The " oratorio mind " must have been ingrained in him from the beginning. Bishop Blomfield had given him half a sovereign and his blessing for writing an anthem when he was still a choir-boy. It was his first professional earnings and a temptation. For a time he turned out, true to his environment, hymns and anthems and occasionally some sentimental, semi-secular

[1] See *Gilbert and Sullivan Journal*, January 1926.

songs. He went to Leipzig as the chosen of seventeen candidates for the Mendelssohn Scholarship. When he returned he became a church organist and made a fair living. And then he rebelled. Just when it seemed that an English Mendelssohn had arrived on the scene he rebelled against the old school and its dullness. The Victorian age was not to be weaned from its idols easily. Sullivan, to be frank, was not cast in the heroic mould, and he was not an idol-smasher himself. He simply drifted away. But it was the throw of a gambler. He left the one established " market " for his wares for one which was at that time undeveloped and hazardous. But Sullivan was by nature a bit of a gambler. I bring in this aspect of his character entirely inoffensively. It is an aspect that may have had a subtle influence on him as a composer. Nothing pleased him more than a friendly game of poker. At times he could plunge pretty heartily too. Gilbert, I am told, held cards in distaste, and if he had friends at home or if he was invited out, the pleasures that attracted him most were those of bright conversation.

Sullivan was no musical landmark. I refuse to rank him, taking his music as a whole, as a first-class composer. But he has claims to greatness. It may be doubted whether his lasting influence on stage music has been profound. He lifted it, of course, to a much higher level, but it was a level to which his successors had not the gifts to aspire. Edward German was, artistically speaking, his one son and heir, and that son and heir, again artistically speaking, went out of business uncommonly early. Sullivan's influence on stage music is represented mainly by his own music only. But in the meantime he had used the stage as an educational agent. He awakened a popular appreciation of better-class music by the help of the operas. He first quickened the pulse of the people by the sound of enchanting melody. And that was something. The theatre in his time had not a name for refinement. Gilbert and Sullivan were the first crusaders for a clean and wholesome stage, and the standard which they set not only made it clean and wholesome then, but they made play-going a popular and respectable pastime.

By extraction—and I shall be introducing this fact later in another connection—Sullivan was half Irishman and half Englishman. He was thus a "rebel" by instinct, and he had also that rather English insularity of taste, that dislike of any dominance of the "foreigner." Before it was too late he went back to bedrock. Study the old English music—the music of Purcell and Morley and Byrd. Nothing that you find in it is more characteristic than its well-marked rhythms and its refreshing melody. And Sullivan's music, written in a much later age, is distinguished by those very qualities. It was with their clear-cut rhythms and delicious tunefulness that the old masters made their appeal, and by reverting to first principles, their descendant found his way just as surely to the heart of the

99

people. Of course, he could go further, and he did go further, than they had gone. He built on the solid ecclesiastical music he had known in his boyhood. He had in his hands a mastery of vocal and choral technique. But there can be no doubt as to his models. It may be true that he rested on the old masters unconsciously. That he divined or discovered their secret somehow is a matter not open to question.

What Sullivan did was without doubt an achievement. But it must be confessed that ever since his critical estimators have done him less justice. The trouble was that, by straying from the true path, he lost caste with the academicals, and it has remained the habit in certain quarters to regard his music superciliously. The old Mendelssohn scholar, with the promise of a classic reputation before him, had taken the wrong turning, and henceforth he could do little right. The charge of " untimely tunefulness " was laid against his " Martyr of Antioch " and " The Golden Legend." Fault had to be found somewhere. " The art form of both author and composer has been lowered, instead of raised, since the establishment of that union which, commercially speaking, has proved so lucrative," said one writer in a critical journal after the production of " Patience." The phrase certainly carried a sting. There was also the critic who dealt with " The Mikado." " The characters," he affirmed sententiously, " are not amusing." The academicals had their biggest revenge when they labelled Sullivan the English

Offenbach. It was a cruel jibe, and one which he resented, though it was fatuously silly.

Gilbertianism, I said at the outset, is in essence topsy-turvydom. For that reason it seemed difficult to argue that we had the compleat Gilbertian in Sullivan. But I am now inclined to withdraw this qualification. Gilbert satirised social conventions by turning them upside down and wrong way about. Sullivan did much for the health of music by twisting some cherished musical conventions awry. Above all there was the old, old convention that no attractive music could ever spring from this tight little island. There was also that terrible Victorian convention, the Handel tradition. Sullivan gave us (in his operas) music that was brighter and lighter, much less sanctimonious in sentiment, much less organistic in style. And in that way he helped to finish off a disastrous blight. For his service in knocking that old gentleman off his throne, I bow to him " most politely, most politely."

CHAPTER XI

THE MAGICAL SPRING

WHERE did Sullivan find his tunes ? I have been asked this question frequently. To me it seems like asking how water gets into or out of the spring. It is the nature of water to do so, just as it is the nature of grass to grow green, the flower to open to the sun, the nightingale to sing. Sullivan wrote tunes because tune-making was part of his nature and the breath of his being. Good tunes welled from him as water wells from the spring. It was the same thing exactly.

Sullivan, as we have just seen, was born into a musical environment. He was saturated in music from infancy. He was attending the military band rehearsals conducted by his father when most children of his age were beginning to be at home in the nursery. In musical matters he was a precocious youngster. Long before he had reached his teens he could play many instruments and read most music by sight. At the age of thirteen he sat down one day and wrote for his father's band the full score of a march which he had heard but which had not been published. The art of odd instrumental effects was a trick he learnt in his childhood. Then he had that invaluable experience as a boy chorister in the Chapel Royal. If we have given Robertson less than his due for his influence on Gilbert, we have failed also in the case of Helmore, that devoted choirmaster who guided the young Sullivan and gave him the choral groundwork that was of immeasurable service later on at the Savoy. Under him the lad became " soaked " in ecclesiastical music. Sullivan began to write his own small compositions, he assisted Helmore in the harmonisation of hymn-tunes, and he caught his Mentor's enthusiasm for the introduction of Gregorian chants in the Church of England. When he returned from Leipzig at the age of eighteen he brought three things with him—a solid grounding in the classical traditions, the conviction that English music badly needed lifting out of a rut, and the score of his fine incidental music to " The Tempest."

I have recapitulated these biographical details simply to show that his musical education was continuous and thorough. I may have shown also by inference that, although he passed through the various musical grades, his only schooling in essentially popular music, such as presumably a military band would provide, occurred in his earliest years. By all the laws of development he should have found his mark in the writing of oratorio and symphony. After all, in estimating what he did and what he might have done, we have to remember that he was the child of his own generation. English music had fallen to its lowest ebb. Oratorio was not merely a vogue but a blight. Covent Garden seldom rose above the levels of Balfe and Donizetti. The atmosphere of popular entertainment was rank and unpleasant. The ballads that the public loved were mainly soulful clap-trap. It is little wonder that the music he wrote throughout his life showed the same sentimental leanings. Early in his career he was frankly imitative in his forms of work and in his style. The " Tempest " music was as Mendelssohnian as one would expect from a Mendelssohn scholar. But before it was too late he escaped from the quicksands. He was influenced, as we have seen, by the old English composers, and he became interested in the best light French and Italian music of Monsigny, Grétry and Delayrac. During the " Patience " period, it has been revealed, he was studying these models very diligently, and they may have given an added nimbleness and lightness to his own musical style.[1]

We have seen that Gilbert was in many ways a paradox. We may now have seen that Sullivan, in going contrary to the lines environment and training seemed to have laid down for him, was also a paradox. Between the two men there was one other point of similarity. Gilbert always yearned to get to what he called serious writing. He may have had ambitions in excess of his powers. Sullivan also wanted to strike a loftier note, though there is

[1] See article by Andrew de Ternant, *Musical Times*, December 1924.

less evidence in his case that he was rebellious that fate, backed by ample financial compensations, kept him pinned to an apparently lowlier plane. In what measure he might have succeeded we may consider in a later chapter. We know that after " Princess Ida " was produced he was writing that he had " come to the end of his tether " in this line of work, and that for a time, at any rate, he was going to do " no more comic opera." That resolution was broken almost before the ink with which it was written was dry. He was soon at work on " The Mikado," followed by " The Yeomen of the Guard " and " The Gondoliers." And nothing he might have written in a different vein could have been so profitable in its immediate rewards or to his lasting reputation.

But where did Sullivan discover his tunes ? That is the matter we set out to discuss. I think the best answer is that most of them came from his heart. They were self-expressive of his own happy spirit. They were the outpourings of a man who saw, not necessarily sermons in trees, not necessarily books in the running brooks, but most certainly " good in everything." Sullivan, an invalid most of his life, had his face ever turned to the sunshine. There was more natural humour in him than there was in Gilbert. There was also in him more charm and graciousness of personality. By birth he was Irish, and accordingly witty ; by descent he was partly Italian, and thus ingrained with a sense of melody ; by up-bringing he was a happy-go-lucky

Englishman. All of this suggests still another paradox. Sullivan, the child of modest Irish parentage, was essentially English. Gilbert, whose family was English and comfortably circumstanced, had something of the dourness of the Scot.

So far as we must trace Sullivan's musical inspiration beyond his own radiant spirit, we may find it in the saturation of musical ideas which occurred in him from his youth upwards, and which yielded in its own time a copious and magical spring. Already we have seen how he reverted in certain of his operatic work to the old English madrigalian forms of Purcell and Morley and Byrd. The greatest examples in this style—they do not stand alone—are the madrigals in " The Mikado " and " Ruddigore." He was also fond of courtly measures like the minuet and the gavotte. We have examples of these old dances in " The Sorcerer," " Ruddigore," " The Gondoliers," and " Utopia." But much more remarkable is the extent to which the ecclesiastical strain gets into the operas. He could no more keep out the ecclesiastical strain than Gilbert could keep out his quaint notion about " equality." This was Sullivan's widow's cruse— to adapt my own simile elsewhere—and it never ran dry.

There is more hymn-tune material concealed in the operas than one would suspect. It is easy enough to identify it, for instance, in the " Hail, Poetry " chorale in " The Pirates of Penzance," in the " I hear a soft note " sestette in " Patience," in

Iolanthe's address to the Lord Chancellor in
" Iolanthe," in Mad Margaret's " To a garden full
of posies " in " Ruddigore," and in the unaccompanied " Eagle high in cloudland soaring " in
" Utopia." These instances are obvious enough.
It is an interesting experiment, nevertheless, to
select an air at random, re-time the medody, reduce
the tempo, and see how easily the air resolves itself
into a hymn. You might begin with the " Silver
Churn " song in " Patience." It is not, on the
face of it, a likely subject for this kind of adaptation,
but if you run some of the repeated notes into one
and play it andante, you will find that it sounds
devout enough for any place of worship.

Now, it is true that one may take any sequence
of notes in the diatonic scale, and with intervals
that are not too wide, and turn them into some
semblance of a hymn-tune. In Sullivan's case
the transformation can often be done rather
effectively. I think there is a sound reason for
this. Sullivan once declared that first of all he
decided in his own mind what rhythm he should
give to a song he had to set, and until he had
decided that matter, and deliberately given it the
most ingenious turn he could, he never gave a
thought to the melody.[1] That came later. In
its embryonic state the melody might or might
not belong to the hymn-tune family, but by the
time the melody had been fitted to the rhythm,
instead of the rhythm fitted to the melody, it was so

[1] See Arthur Lawrence's *Life of Sir Arthur Sullivan.*

emasculated that its ecclesiastical basis could not be recognised.

Sullivan, it has to be remembered, was very partial to the four-bar phrase. He had the " four-bar mind," as many greater composers before him had had, and he was not an innovator who would break from tradition. I am not suggesting that all his melodies fall into these four-bar compartments. I do suggest, however, that this is the plan he usually follows, and it helps to account for what similarity there may be between his melodies and hymn-tunes, which are almost invariably built on the four-bar phrase. Wagner, by whom, unlike most of the composers of the time, he seems not to have been influenced to any degree, probably did more than anyone definitely to break the tradition, and the moderns have completed the process. Sullivan, as a four-bar musician, was merely faithful to his generation. He was faithful to it, moreover, as a diatonic musician, and the absence of numerous chromatics makes his music agreeable to the ear and easy to sing.

A charge that has been laid against him more than once is that of " cribbing." " He himself," one of the best-informed chroniclers of the Savoy operas tells us, " was ever the first to plead guilty to such a soft impeachment." [1] Well, it has been the habit in all ages for composers, as it has been for writers and poets, to take other men's ideas and apply them to their own purposes. Wagner did it,

---

[1] Cellier and Bridgeman in *Gilbert, Sullivan, and D'Oyly Carte.*

and so even, in the sphere of literature, did Shakespeare. If, then, Sullivan stole a few bars, his conscience might have been easy. And, as he said when he was accused of using in " When a Merry Maiden marries " a phrase reminiscent of " Love's Old Sweet Song," a tune he declared he had never heard, its composer and himself had " only eight notes to work upon." In any case, assuming the odds are against him, which they probably are not, he turned a dreadfully banal air into one of rare charm and delicate workmanship.

Certainly he was not a plagiarist in a big way. He had too many ideas of his own to make him a beggar. If he borrowed, as has been alleged, from the old opera bouffe which is now dead and forgotten, he would surely have borrowed also from the old madrigalists on whom he more obviously rested his style. And yet he has never been caught paying them that compliment. He was often, of course, an imitator. There is that clever Handel trio in " Princess Ida." In the same opera there are oddments that savour of Verdi and Mendelssohn and Mozart. But all this, so far from being copy work, is deliberate parody. " That's how it was done " he is saying. The Verdi manner he imitates frequently. We still wait for a musician who can show himself to be as clever an imitator—of Sullivan.

For the most part his " cribs " were from old folk-songs and old airs of the folk-song type. Why should he not give us a dash of Charles Dibdin in

the sailor verse of the " Wandering Minstrel " song
or in the breezy ditty of the " Darned Mounseer " ?
In " The British Tar is a soaring soul " there is
an unmistakable fragment of " Tom Bowling."
" For he is an Englishman " owns obvious parentage to an old sea-shanty. It was a sea-shanty also
which he took for the tune of " I have a song to
sing O ! " Gilbert had taken his metrical style
for this lyric from an old nautical ballad known as
the Dilly Song. Cornish sailors had sung it on his
own yacht—an almost interminable song in the
form of a vocal dialogue for two voices with chorus
repetitions.

First Singer :	Come, and I will sing you.
Second Singer :	What will you sing me ?
First Singer :	I'll sing you two O !
Second Singer :	What is your two O ?
First Singer :	Two of them were lily-white maids
	Dressed all in green O.
Chorus :	One of them is all alone
	And ever will remain so.

This is the second verse, and there are additions to
each verse until it reaches its full length, " I will
sing you twelve O ! " From the religious allusions
at the end it was obviously of some antiquity.
There is sufficient here to show what gave Gilbert
the basic inspiration for the Merryman Song. It
would appear that, when he took the ballad as his
own pattern, he did not necessarily intend that
the musical style should be followed also by his

composer. Sullivan wrestled for a fortnight, including many sleepless nights, over what he called "that blessed jingle." In the end Gilbert hummed the air to him and he was able to go ahead. The song as we know it has a striking resemblance to the shanty, though the melody is richer and the setting, of course, highly ingenious.

Gilbert and Sullivan both understood that the words and music to which the Mikado enters were authentically Japanese. Not until later did they discover—or so the story goes—that in its own land the song they had used had a most unsavoury pedigree.[1] The air of " Behold ! the Lord High Executioner " has a clear relationship (and what a perfect gem of musical satire it is, remembering the antecedents of Ko-Ko !) to that of " A Fine Old English Gentleman." You catch a phrase or two of " The British Grenadiers " in Lord Mount-ararat's " In good King George's glorious days." " Twenty Love-sick Maidens " has some resemblance to the second theme of " Alas ! those chimes " in " Maritana." " I hear a soft note " reminds one of a tune that was once popular for " Lead, Kindly Light." And in the Drawing-room music in " Utopia " there is a snatch of " Johnny, get your gun." [2] I do not suppose that this list is complete. And in any case it is well to be wary. The searcher for these supposed

[1] Shelford Walsh in *Gilbert and Sullivan Jottings.*
[2] The subject of Sullivan's " cribbed tunes " is dealt with by T. T. Champion, *Gilbert and Sullivan Journal,* October 1925.

III

derivations is liable to be assisted by an over-active imagination.

Let us return to the point from which we began. Sullivan was influenced by the grand old master-singers of this land in past generations. He was immersed in music from childhood, and there were folk tunes which, sub-consciously or otherwise, he utilised. The Church music amidst which he grew up gave root and partial direction to his musical style. But, above all, his music came from the heart. It was his own sunny nature that was his chief inspiration. Suffering though he did from chronic ill-health, it has been said of him that " he inspired in all who came into contact with him or his work a spirit of tranquil happiness, an exquisite appreciation of the joy of living." [1] And his music has just those qualities. It is sincere music—no critic has denied it that—because he himself was sincere.

Nature may have her grandest monuments in the frowning peaks. But her handiwork is just as wonderful when we see it revealed in a garden. This must be the measure of Sullivan. Composers there are who tower above him and make him seem a man of small stature. Actually there is no point for comparison. They wrote great music, but he wrote lovely music, as lovely as the flowers that bloom in the spring.

[1] It is a touching thought that this life-long sufferer's last work should have been a Te Deum. It was written when he was a very sick man, in anticipation of the close of the South African War, and was given posthumously at St. Paul's Cathedral in 1902.

CHAPTER XII

TAKING SULLIVAN'S MEASURE

SULLIVAN, it has often been said, did not make the fullest use of his genius. It is urged that he would have done greater work had he cut himself adrift from the stage. The suggestion here is that theatre music is a low order of music, that it has an easy but ephemeral appeal, and that it is an unworthy medium for a front-rank composer. In a book on Gilbert and Sullivan I cannot be expected to subscribe to this opinion. By innuendo, as Shadbolt would say, it pays the operas a compliment. They are the work of a man who was conceivably " too good for the stage."

In some respects the theory is demonstrably wrong. Sullivan's theatre music is not low music. It is, take it all in all, the best popular music that has ever been written, whether for the stage or not for the stage. Nor has it been ephemeral. It has stood an almost day-to-day test, both in the theatre and out of it, for little short of fifty years. It has had a test which has not had to be suffered, for instance, by that great work of Sullivan's in another line, " The Golden Legend." For ten who know

" The Golden Legend " there are thousands who know " The Mikado." If he could have written more oratorio he might have made a greater theoretical reputation, but oratorio is now almost an extinct art form, and it would have been a dead reputation. That is not the case with the operas.

The truth is that a composer of his calibre had never been captured before by the popular stage. (I necessarily distinguish the popular from the grand opera stage, which had had a succession of big men, extending from Mozart to Wagner.) When he entered its service Sullivan was more than a novice. The " Tempest " music, the Irish Symphony, and a host of sentimental ballads, vastly popular in their day, whatever else they may or may not have been, had preceded the writing of " Trial by Jury." And it is of interest to note the other work he was doing when he was composing the operas. " Cox and Box " was his first venture into the comic opera sphere.[1] The " In Memoriam " overture roughly coincided with this important milestone in his career. " The Light of the World," a commonplace oratorio redeemed by at least one great solo, belongs to the period that also produced " Trial by Jury." The year that gave " The Pirates of Penzance " provided also " The Martyr of Antioch," and the year that gave " The Mikado " must have found him at work on " The Golden Legend." Later he became an unofficial musical

[1] *Cox and Box* was done in collaboration with Burnand in 1867. *The Contrabandista* with the same collaborator appeared in the same year.

laureate who wrote music associated with great national events or the ceremonial affairs of Royalty. The popular stage certainly never had at its service a musician of such versatility or of such prestige.

Sullivan was once labelled the English Offenbach.[1] It took many years to free his name from that malicious sobriquet. Gilbert, one remembers, has been called the English Aristophanes. On the whole Gilbert's burden seems to have been the more senseless. Only a " fascination frantic " for labels would cause anyone to grope back for comparisons into the classic ages. In any case Gilbert had neither the coarseness nor the mythological bent of Aristophanes. The English Offenbach myth is merely stupid. The English Schubert would be much nearer the truth. Offenbach had an undeniable turn of melody, and he could often write dramatically, which is what his supposed protégé could do but rarely. Sullivan's muse was more refined, much more consistently elegant, and the plays for which he wrote had an incomparably higher literary quality. Offenbach's librettists, Meilhac and Halévy, cannot be mentioned in the same breath with Gilbert. In any case the idioms of the two men were utterly dissimilar. One does not recall that Offenbach ever wrote a " Golden Legend." One doubts, indeed, whether this " merry clown " would ever have had the depth for it, or for anything beyond tickling the ears of the

---

[1] This absurd title was given him by G. A. Macfarren in an article in the *Encyclopædia Britannica*.

groundlings.[1] "The Tales of Hoffman" alone has saved his reputation, and that work belongs, after all, more to real opera than to his own opera bouffe.

It is a difficult matter to find Sullivan's true place in the musical hierarchy. We know that in every field he entered he was as sure of himself as he was thorough. The inspiration may run thin now and again, but in the workmanship there is nothing rough and tumble, nothing superficial. The trouble is that there are many Sullivans. There is the Sullivan of " The Lost Chord " and " The Absent-Minded Beggar." Here we have him as the composer of popular songs which haunted their day and generation. This side of him is of minor account. " Sweethearts " and many of his other drawing-room ballads are better forgotten. The songs by which he may be more worthily remembered are those like " Orpheus and his Lute " and the deeply-moving " Thou art passing hence." There is the Sullivan of the part-songs—and these include many beautiful things. There is the Sullivan of the hymns, of which there is none better than the so-called war-march of the Church Militant, his St. Gertrude tune to " Onward, Christian Soldiers." There is the Sullivan of " The Mikado." Here we know him best of all. There is the Sullivan of " Ivanhoe." Here we have him realising a life ambition, at least as regards stage work, and writing

---

[1] It was Lord Beaconsfield who called Offenbach a " merry clown in the service of Napoleon III."

grand opera. " Ivanhoe," which is supposed not
to have been a success, had a longer consecutive
run than any other grand opera has had, and the fact
that he was not encouraged to write a successor to
it was due to circumstances for which, as composer,
he was not responsible.[1]   And then there is the
Sullivan of " The Golden Legend."   This work
I have used to typify his greatest achievements away
from the stage.

> " Take of these elements all that is fusible,
>   Melt them all down in a pipkin or crucible "—

and is the " residuum " a Sullivan who, working
consistently along the higher levels of abstract
music, might have taken his place amongst the
immortals of his calling ?

It is to be feared that something would be lacking.
It is certainly not that his technical equipment was inadequate.   Sullivan was a fount of ideas, greatly gifted
as a melodist, quite as greatly gifted as a rhythmist.
He was a master of vocal part-writing.   He had a
remarkable sense of orchestration.   He might, so
far as the ability to contrive bizarre effect was concerned, have rivalled Berlioz in " sound and fury."
He did not do so because he had no leanings that
way.   He could touch his music with all the more
surface emotions.   He could make it humoursome,

---

[1] *Ivanhoe*, produced in 1891, opened Richard D'Oyly Carte's Royal
English Opera House, now the Palace Theatre. It was intended to
form part of a repertory programme, but there was no new opera to
replace it, and this proved disastrous to the enterprise. *Ivanhoe* itself
had a run of over five months.

daintily and graciously sentimental, or frankly joyous. At times it is the music of a man whose nature had been stirred deeply. The " In Memoriam " overture, written under the shadow of his father's death, is suffused with filial grief and piety. In " Thou art passing hence," written after the death of his brother, he is moved to the same noble utterance, though the work is a smaller thing. The spirit of lament, whatever the cause that inspired it, broods over the lovely slow movement of the Irish Symphony. In his music, as we have seen, there is often the devotional strain. In part it reflected the lines of his training, but in part also it was the reflection of a man of reverent faith, a man in whom the spiritual impulses were strong.

We get most things in his music—except real drama and passion. Neither in the operas nor elsewhere does he strike the really incisive note, the note of dramatic intensity, the note of challenging vigour. There are no soul-surging emotions welling up and demanding expression. Other hands might delineate the human storms and tempests. The scene which he sketches is nearly always that of a fair and beautiful landscape. Carrying forward the simile, it may be at times a landscape with the more sombre autumn tints, but the atmosphere remains restful, the spirit uncomplaining. Lovely it may be, but so far as it purports to be a mirror of life and nature, the image is hardly complete.

Sullivan had the musical defects of his personal

qualities. Life, to this unconquerable soul, was wonderfully good. Apart from health, it had given him all that he could ask for, and he accepted fame and fortune with modesty and with contentment of spirit. In his heart there were no enmities—nor were there many passionate yearnings. Kindly-natured as he was, a man of the warmest sympathies in his own circle, we never gather that he had any promptings to be a crusader for the social betterment of the people at large. If his professional path had been less easy, if he had had to fight adversity, the music that came out of him might have been of a profounder quality. He never had to suffer the neglect that was the lot of Mozart or Schubert, the embitterments of Berlioz or Wagner, the mental cloudiness of Beethoven or Schumann. Essentially an impressionable man, he would certainly have been a better musician had he had to battle, and battle hard, for recognition. That, indeed, is the lot of mankind, even those who are naturally gifted.

It has been said of Sullivan, more than a little uncharitably, that he had been blinded by gold-dust, and that his ambitions towards abstract music were warped by the lavish rewards which he received from the Savoy. This is the supercilious attitude of those who have held that there is something derogatory in a front-rank composer writing for the popular stage. It may be true that it would take an heroic man deliberately to leave an assured field for one which offered problematical honour and far more problematical pay. But it is not true that success made him indolent. He had a prodigious output. The operas, the non-theatrical music which he wrote, and his work as a festival conductor kept him constantly busy. Nor did success make him apathetic. The ambition towards more serious work remained with him to the end of his days.

What rank Sullivan would have taken had he been mainly a symphony and oratorio composer must remain a matter of pure speculation. We know from the work that he did do that he showed wonderful promise amounting to actual performance. But there were two reasons that conceivably might have hampered his development. One was the lack of that power to write trenchantly and dramatically. A composer who cannot ring the changes on all the human emotions can never achieve absolute greatness. The other reason, and a more curious one, was that he was constitutionally of the limpet type. It was when clinging to somebody else, and when in association with somebody who, as it were, kindled the imaginative fires in him, that he had his best inspiration. It was Gilbert who invoked nearly all the best music he did. The partner's influence was almost mesmeric. It may be true that " The Golden Legend " was Sullivan's unaided work, but that was an exception that proved the rule, and there was only one " Golden Legend." There were a number of operas. There were also those operas which were not written in association with Gilbert. Sullivan had to find some other

Moses to strike the rock for him—and the substitute could never quite do the trick. There is enough here to make us wonder whether the composer, with all his gifts and technique, could have carved his own lone furrow up the slopes of Parnassus.

Sullivan was really a Peter Pan composer. That is the worst that can be said of him. Musically he never grew up. It was a case—deliberately or otherwise—of arrested development. Study his earlier and his later music, and you have to concede that, while his technical standard at the beginning was a high one, it never got really perceptibly higher. A tremendous gap divides the Wagner of " Rienzi " and the " Flying Dutchman " from the Wagner of " Tristan and Isolde " and " The Mastersingers." An immense growth has taken place between the Verdi of " Il Trovatore " and the Verdi of " Otello." There is a vast difference between the Elgar of " King Olaf " and the Elgar of " The Dream of Gerontius." With all these men the years brought profound development. Sullivan was certainly not of their mettle, but if we limit our comparisons to his own sphere, we have reason to question whether the music of " Utopia," surer and more freely endowed though it may be, is of any materially higher level than that of " Trial by Jury." Between these two works was, or should have been, the fruitful growth of eighteen years.

Gilbert's rôle, as we have seen, was first and foremost that of a humorist, the man whose job it was to make the people laugh. We discount his claims to be a serious dramatist, but we acknowledge that as a humorist, wonderfully well equipped for his task, his peer has not been seen on the popular stage. Sullivan's rôle was that of the musician of the people. He may have been more than that, but he was certainly no less, and he also placed a superb equipment at the service of the popular stage. We need not trouble if he fails to gain admission to the circle of the supremely great composers. We know that he has been lauded truly as "the sweetest singer of his generation." The ghosts of some of the immortals would covet such an epitaph.

CHAPTER XIII

CONCERNING THE LADIES

GILBERT, it has often been said, never spoilt his stage women by any excessive flattery. Not only do I hold this to be true, but it has seemed to me that the weakness of his characterisation of women is a flaw in the operas, inasmuch as it stamps them with an age that the freshness of the story and music disguises. Gilbert's women are terribly Victorian. Ko-Ko, Pooh-Bah, Jack Point, Don Alhambra, and many other male characters are clear-cut types, each distinctive and definite, and as such they belong to the stage. It never occurs to us to classify them as belonging to the past or the present. But it is not so with the ladies. They are all so much of a pattern. They " date " themselves— and the operas with them—as the relics of a past generation.

Speaking generally, Gilbert drew his women-folk from two models only, and in real life their types are almost forgotten. You cannot escape from his simpering innocents or from his man-trapping spinsters. They positively litter the ground. The younger ones have little personality and less self-dependence. It would be difficult to picture one of them going into business or setting up house as a bachelor girl. Seemingly they all have pretty voices, they dress with taste, and they look bewitchingly charming. But how terribly conventional they are and how exasperatingly " according to plan " ! Empty-headed creatures most of them are, just casting a demure eye when a possible husband appears on the scene, and looking as if they might faint becomingly when the silly fellow seems inclined to propose. It does not exhaust the list by any means, but you need only take Yum-Yum, Casilda, Patience, Rose Maybud, and Elsie Maynard. They are mostly of the clinging type whose sense of decorum is stifling.

Of course, they have youth on their side, they look very pretty, and the rays of romance play about them divinely. In these respects they may leave the disappointed old maids at a complete disadvantage. Why is it that Gilbert, with his inventive fund of humour, so often makes a mock of those pitiable creatures who are, and sometimes plainly announce that they are, on the bargain-counters of marriage ? Socially, he cannot have been brought into touch much with these petulant spinsters, and the married women in his operas, though they may be of no outstanding interest, are usually drawn with respect. Lady Jane and Katisha are the best or the worst of those sorry examples. Lady Jane's chase after Bunthorne is not edifying comedy, and the words put into her mouth are a trifle cheap, though the worst instance of this the beauty of the music disguises. My own Victorian recollections do not tell me that maiden ladies used to flaunt their caps with such flagrant despair.

Some of the younger ladies are almost pre-historic in their primness. You will remember the embarrassment of the daughters of Major-General Stanley. Each has taken off a shoe with a view to a paddle, and when a man catches her in this shocking state of deshabille, the poor creature hops round on one foot disconcertedly. Then there is Patience. She, of course, is a freak. She has never heard of love— and her age is between eighteen and twenty. And yet in the arts of coquetry she seems to be a fairly promising pupil. She coquets with Archibald Grosvenor, but it has to be a strictly proper affair, with a safe distance between them. Let him advance one step, and as a good and pure woman, she warns him, she screams ! At all costs Patience must be a perfect young lady.

But the most terrible survival is Rose Maybud. She is the bashful maiden—though one never believes her supposed bashfulness for a moment— whose every action is regulated by a code of etiquette devised by no less an authority than a Lady Mayoress. She may not hint or whisper or point. Her " hallowed volume " forbids it. It also forbids biting the nails or eating peas with a knife. How should a nicely bred girl receive a young man's approaches ? How should she accept an offer of marriage ? Should she allow herself to be kissed ? The guide and monitor has its counsel for every occasion.

And, really, if there is a girl who could find her way about the world without a book of etiquette, that girl is Rose Maybud. As a shrewd weigher-up of matrimonial opportunities she has hardly an equal. In the course of one act we hear that she had given her heart in turn to three different men, and one of them, Richard Dauntless, she is anxious to leave because he is a poor mariner and has no " fat oxen and many sheep and swine," like Robin Oakapple. One would have supposed that such cynical gyrations in search of the main chance were also " contrary to etiquette."

Opinions will always vary as to the most likeable figure on the feminine side of the operas. My own choice will not be one that has, perhaps, the widest acceptance, for at no cost will I have Elsie Maynard. I cannot forgive her for the seemingly callous way in which she turns her back on the companion of her heart-aching days. It is Jack Point's fate, we know, that focuses the interest when the curtain is falling, and possibly that is why her indifference is not so glaring. Of course, a young lady has a right to wed a man whose neck is half on the block if she wants to, and she must be allowed to jilt if she pleases. But Elsie, doting in the arms of her groom, has no thought of pity and no word of comfort for the heart-broken jester, and she offers him nothing more than a glance.

To my mind Gilbert's best-drawn woman is Katisha. She is an unlovable being, the man-eating tigress after her prey, with the jealousy of a cat, the spite of a viper, and an overbearing manner that can quell a Mikado. But it is her domineering personality that makes her dramatically strong. Katisha confesses that she is an acquired taste, that she has to train a man to love her, and that the training takes years. Knowing the lady—at least from the safe side of the footlights—one thinks this is not improbable. Ko-Ko she certainly tames in a much shorter time, but in the special circumstances the victim is not displeased with his bargain. Solely on the comedy side the character is one of the best the dramatist drew. That line about the left shoulder blade that is a miracle of loveliness is surely one of the wittiest things in the operas.

In these plays Princess Ida stands aloof and apart. She resembles a Greek goddess, a classic figure of icy insensibility, a humourless creature embittered by her obsession for women's rights. Iolanthe, of course, is much, much more human. Yet she, too, is rather remote and unreal, a lonely and a tragic soul in a fantastic environment. But amongst the women the outstanding tragic figure is surely Mad Margaret. The appearance of the distracted girl in her white dress and her straw-bedecked hair is dramatic—and all the more dramatic because she is alone on the stage. " Crazy Meg " has a haunting ballad, and then comes her splendid scene, the wit never strained into falsity, with Rose Maybud. It is a dramatic license, and a deplorable one, when this Ophelia-like girl, a splendid dramatic and vocal part, is transformed later into a kind of blameless Puritan's Daughter. The change from tragedy into bathos is altogether too sweeping.

One of the most human of Gilbert's women is Phœbe. She has a wondrous fund of affection and a sense of sacrifice. It is a pity that her duet with the gaoler should be an excuse for comic by-play. The ogling of the eyes, the stroking of the scrubby beard, and the other oddities of sentimental silliness tend to clash with the motive of what is, in essence, a yearning love song. Study the words of " Were I thy bride," and one sees that the girl is in a dreamy reverie, the central figure in which is, not Shadbolt at all, but Colonel Fairfax. She is picturing the boundless depth of her love were her affections accepted. For the sake of the man she loves, and while her heart is breaking, she enters into the loathsome pretence of weedling the uncouth and lugubrious gaoler. Even to touch him at such a moment, much more to caress him, must be repulsive. She goes through the grim farce at the call of an unrequited passion. Shadbolt is such a poor fool that he does not see that the feeling behind her words is that of sarcastic disgust. In happier circumstances Phœbe would be a fine little woman with a loyalty as staunch as steel.

> " Were I thy bride,
>   Then all the world beside
>   Were not too wide
>   To hold my wealth of love,
>   Were I thy bride."

CONCERNING THE LADIES

Yet, for the most attractive women of all, commend me to Tessa and Gianetta. Essentially feminine and lovable as they are—and this is abundantly shown by their songs—they have also engaging self-reliance and spirit. Each has a mind of her own, and when she puts her little foot down, the gondolier has need to be wary. Each has a brisk touch of temper. Each is alert to the chances of social advancement. And each has the pluck to venture over the vasty seas in order to keep a happy-go-lucky husband under her eye. Nanki-Poo, Colonel Fairfax and Luiz may have made a good choice in their brides, but I personally would envy them less than I would envy Marco and Giuseppe. They at least were married to pals. My own favourite is Gianetta. She is the gentler of the two, and one cannot see her, like Tessa, turning a taunting wit at the Grand Inquisitor. Giuseppe may yet have his hands full with that little spitfire.

Somehow I can imagine that Tessa and Gianetta, if they came to live with us in these times, would promptly have their hair shingled and revel in a round of golf every morning. At all events they would make themselves a match for the girl of to-day. The Patience type would be left simpering over her antimacassars.

CHAPTER XIV

RANK AND RANKERS

In our discussion on the women characters we saw that they were usually drawn from two or three stock patterns, and these mainly obsolete patterns. It was suggested, on the other hand, that the men conformed to no particular model and to no particular age, and that we could regard them as stage types entirely. I propose now to consider a few of the male rôles in the operas. It will not be pretended that these will be accepted as the most popular parts. Such a selection would have to be in any case a personal one, and it would depend whether the standard of judgment was to be a part demanding rollicking comedy, the nicer shades of emotion, or the gift of good singing. If a vote were taken I suppose that Jack Point would be established as the most popular figure by a fairly big margin. Whom the second best would be I am less certain about, though I would risk the prophecy that a democratic ballot would assign that position to Ko-Ko, followed by Bunthorne, followed in turn possibly by the Duke of Plaza-Toro. With all of these I am dealing in other chapters. The question of popularity does not enter into these further reflections.

My own idea is that Pooh-Bah is the greatest man in the operas.[1] He is a great character even if he is so utterly impossible. I am not referring to his weightiness in avoidupois. Nevertheless, there is something awesome in the very rotundity of the man, in his almost noble ponderosity. Pooh-Bah has added a name to the currency of speech. We all know the men whose life ambition it is to have a finger in every pie in the making. They are to be found in business life and in all kinds of "movements." The multiplicity of rôles which they collect for themselves does credit to their versatility and to their energy. We call them Pooh-Bahs, but whether the compliment is meant to be happy or not, the title is usually wrongly applied. In the first place the real Pooh-Bah has an eye only to profitable sinecures in which enthusiasm would be misplaced. And in the accumulation of offices, and most of them highly paid ones, this arch pluralist leaves his human imitators gasping. He is a Prime Minister, he is a Lord Mayor, and he is an Archbishop. That is not at all bad as a beginning. In all, you may be surprised to learn, he is credited with holding about twenty-six different appointments, and probably there will be additions to the collection, for we find no

---

[1] In *Sir William Gilbert: A Study of Modern Satire*, Professor Isaac Goldberg, an American writer, also describes the character of Pooh-Bah as " perhaps the greatest single creation of Gilbert."

evidence that any "economy" zealots have been battering at the doors of the Titipuan Treasury.

How on earth did he obtain all these lucrative honours when all the other officers of State refused to serve under Ko-Ko? Pooh-Bah was a tremendous swell. He describes himself as of "pre-Adamite ancestral descent." He could trace his ancestry back "to a protoplasmal primordial atomic globule." In a land devoted to ancestral worship these would surely be sufficient qualifications for preferment. In times not long ago a good pedigree was alleged to be a precious useful political stepping-stone even in England. Beyond these Pooh-Bah seems to have no valid claim at all for the titles and the stipends that have crowded upon him. Not for a moment would he pass for a man of "push and go." He is very much the opposite. Nor has he the small talk that would make him a court favourite of the Mikado. Least of all is he troubled with brains. A Cabinet Minister many times over, and presumably knowing a trick or two worth knowing, he is as guileless and as gullible as a simpleton. One would have thought he would have had the craft, this many-sided man of affairs, never to have fallen into the sorry muddles of a little upstart like Ko-Ko. Pooh-Bah lets Ko-Ko do all the thinking. Ko-Ko is the sole author of the scheme for a mock execution, and Pooh-Bah lumbers into it, too dull and indolent to realise that, though a great officer of State, he is becoming an accomplice in the beheading of the Heir-

Apparent. The Pooh-Bahs so called in real life, to give them their due, are not witless or drowsy. The use of the name pays small tribute to their sagacity and enterprise.

Pooh-Bah is not merely the master pluralist. He is the embodiment of meanliness and mercenary greed. It is avarice that is his chief characteristic, and if he is to be taken as a type at all, he is the type of the boundlessly avaricious man, and not primarily the man who revels in an array of offices concentrated in his own person. The " insatiable ambition " he talks about has a cash basis only. He has no ambition for power solely as power. Still less has he the born intriguer's craving to get all the strings into his grip. To one of his sluggish mind the burden of responsibility would be insupportable. He is an Olympian who grovels to pocket the coppers. Graft is the breath of life to him, and to finger a bribe, much as he professes that it revolts him, he can endure insults with a smirking complacency and a " mortified pride." Of course, there is no one quite like Pooh-Bah in real life, or even could be, and he is a great character mainly in the sense that he is so sublimely and monumentally original.

Let me now bring down your mind to a much lower plane. I want to re-introduce you to Private Willis, B Company, 1st Grenadier Guards. You will agree that here we have " quite a different sort of person." He is the sort of person who has his job to do, who finds it a profitless and wearisome job, but who does it and never complains. "Iolanthe" could run its course without the appearance of this dutiful sentry, but what a dash of colour his red uniform gives to the scene, and what a symbol of plain common sense his tall figure is amid this crazy make-believe near Parliament Square! What Private Willis has to say is negligible. Like a good soldier, he never speaks until he is spoken to, and then he raps out his answer crisply and smartly. He is too well drilled to chatter or to mind anybody's business but his own. It is no concern of his if folk want to make fools of themselves. Standing there by his box, almost statuesque in his indifference to the tantrums of the Peers and the tears of the Fairies, he looks as solid, and as sane, as the British Constitution. As a foil his inclusion was a stroke of genius.

At heart he is a cynic. We know that from his song. It is only in the moonlight hours, and when the clock tower at Westminster looks down on a deserted scene, that he " lets himself go."

> " When all night long a chap remains
> On sentry go, to chase monotony
> He exercises of his brains,
> That is, assuming that he's got any.
> Though never nurtured in the lap
> Of luxury, yet I admonish you,
> I am an intellectual chap,
> And think of things that would astonish you."

What, one wonders, are the things this intellectual chap is thinking of when the paragons of British legislation consort with charming ladies with white dresses and wings, and when it transpires that these gossamer creatures are Parliamentary dictators? From his attitude of boredom, one might take it that he sees nothing startling about it, and that incidents of this kind are part of the humdrum sights of the day. About an M.P.'s intelligence he never had an exalted opinion. And he has come to the conclusion that in political matters mankind are very like sheep. From birth on they just stray into one or other of the political folds and stay there. He typifies the " man in the street." He has shrewd ideas of his own, but as nobody wants to hear them, he just thinks the more and carries on with his job. He stands there with two feet firm on the ground. And in this respect he differs from everyone else in this deliciously fanciful opera.

Let me take as my third figure His Distinction the Grand Inquisitor. He typifies common sense in " The Gondoliers" in much the same manner that Private Willis typifies it in " Iolanthe." Nor is this the sole resemblance between the two men. In their vastly different ranks and spheres they are the lonely and scantily-heeded representatives of constituted authority. They are stubborn material-ists in a world of make-believe inconsequence. Private Willis keeps his thoughts locked up in his own manly person. Don Alhambra is more articu-late. We are inclined to regard him too much from the aspect of an unctuous and very dignified person. We do him less than justice when we ignore his outstanding quality. He is a man of the most marvellous tact.

The Don is really far too kind for his job. He is neither autocratic nor in the very least inquisitive. A Grand Inquisitor of Spain would not ordinarily allow a Venetian boatman to slap him on the back, call him " his man," and affront him with pernicious Republican doctrines. Far more likely is it that he would summon his bodyguard, produce the keys of the torture chamber, and jingle them with an ominous meaning. And if the offender had been consigned to custody forthwith he would not have been supplied with a stock of the illustrated papers. " Bless my heart ! how unfortunate ! " exclaims this tender-hearted functionary when he hears these sturdy Republican professions from a gondolier who is possibly a King. It reminds one of the Mikado's " Dear, dear, dear ! this is very tiresome " when he learns of the supposed execution of his only son, the Heir-Apparent.

This " how unfortunate " attitude is rather characteristic of the Grand Inquisitor. He does not storm or scatter anathema. Life, he reminds us, is one closely complicated tangle, and he tries to unravel its dilemmas in the most conciliatory manner possible. Certain novel adventures in the Baratarian Court have disturbed his sense of the fitness of things. He is too courteous to condemn them in unmeasured language. Experiments of this kind " won't do," but why they won't do is explained, quite nicely and persuasively, by the aid of a parable. This was the story of the misguided Monarch whose heart " found a place for all the erring human race and every wretched fellow." The scheme would not work. For tactfulness this diplomatic pointing of a great truth takes a good deal of beating.

The Grand Inquisitor, as I have said, is a representative of constituted authority. He is also the representative of the *status quo*. He is no believer in these new-fangled notions about equality. They are not practicable and they are not proper. In all courts there are distinctions that must be observed. By all means let an Archbishop play leap-frog if he wants to unloosen his limbs—but for the sake of the proprieties do let him choose men of his own station for playmates. This is not altogether a question of snobbery. The social order may be shaken to its roots by mishaps that may occur during the mixing of men of high and lowlier breeding. He foresees one of these possible inelegancies plainly:

" You wouldn't have a Lord High Chancellor play leap-frog with his own cook. Why not ? Because a Lord High Chancellor is a personage of great dignity, who should never, under any circumstances, place himself in the position of being told to tuck in his tuppenny except by noblemen of his own rank. A Lord High Archbishop, for instance, might tell a Lord High Chancellor to tuck in his tuppenny, but certainly not a cook, gentlemen, certainly not a cook."

Challenge this theory if you will—and it is not so easily challenged—you certainly cannot question the infinite tact of the Grand Inquisitor. He is just as tactful when he is demonstrating the falsity of giving everyone an ornamental title and placing him on a pinnacle. The thing will not work. The Don is the owner of the one logical head in the play. He is far more logical than is, for instance, that affected little gadabout, the Duke of Plaza-Toro. He could have withered the Baratarian theorists, this man of worldly wisdom, with a mighty contempt. Actually he blows over the crazy house of cards with the urbanity of a kindly and irreproachably-mannered philosopher. As a Gilbert character he stands very high.

And then there is Wilfred Shadbolt. He also is a type. He is no Private Willis, a man who sings his song, who does his job, and who never complains. He typifies rather those in whom there is the smouldering discontent that destiny should have bound and chained them to the humdrum things. On the world's stage they would play a more congenial and a loftier part. They would shine in it as other men shine, and they would have the homage, these idle dreamers of dreams, that is rendered to gift and position. This Shadbolt did not become a head-jailor because he liked head-jailing. He did not become an assistant-tormentor because he liked assistant-tormenting. Fate sent him to the Tower to work the rack and the thumbscrew, and one has a shrewd idea that he can rack and thumbscrew in a conscientious, workman-like fashion. But it is clear that, apart altogether from any feelings of compassion, he is not in love with his job. The monotony of it has soured him and made him morose. And the world has only scoffs when a jailer, who has a heart like most men, though it is hidden under a grimy exterior, is the victim of an unrequited passion. Is it to be wondered at that he is gnawed by jealousy? He admits it, and he admits also, this assistant-tormentor in the torments of love, that his suspicious nature has lured him to peep through the keyholes.

It is Jack Point who stirs the embers of discontent into a flame. The ungainly, lumbering fool, the embodiment of dirt and drabness, would be himself a light-hearted jester. Jack Point has a good post—the irony of it!—and good cause to be merry. Yet he has a pretty wit too, an airy and a joysome wit, spiced with anecdotes of prison cells and the torture chamber, and delicate enough to be tried on the sorry creatures consigned to his keeping. It should not be difficult, so this melancholy numskull sees it, to become a good jester. And, for reasons of his own, Jack Point offers to teach him the tricks of the trade, and to make him without a peer in his calling. The whole affair is absurd. And yet it rings true as a satire on a great human folly. It is the " second chance " doctrine in a humorous form, the doctrine that, if only one were given one's time over again, one's life would be ordered on a vastly different plan. It matters not that the dreamer is utterly unsuited for the part to which he aspires. In essentials Wilfred Shadbolt, the hang-dog jailor who would be a merry wag, is companion to the clerk who would be a social " lion," the village debater who would be the modern Demosthenes, and the girl typist who sighs to become the gilded heroine herself on " the pictures."

Last of all in this masculine gallery I take old Sergeant· Meryll. What a lovable figure he is! Conspirator he may be, for it is due to his treacherous act that the Tower's execution block is cheated of its victim, Colonel Fairfax. But this same Colonel Fairfax had twice saved his life in the country's battles, and the old soldier is ready to be faithless to his wardership if he may serve and save him in turn, though his own grey head may pay the forfeit. Meryll typifies the virtue of gratitude in a practical shape. It is a virtue which shines through the stories of these operas but rarely. The veteran saves his skin—but at the cost of marrying an elderly lady and thus sealing her lips. We need offer him no commiserations on that. Dame Carruthers should make a splendid mate for this sturdy old yeoman. Many contented years may they spend under the sombre walls of old London Tower!

CHAPTER XV

THOUGHTS ABOUT JACK POINT

Sometimes I think we overlook one important matter in studying the character of Jack Point in " The Yeomen of the Guard." In a rough and ready way : how old was the jester ? Upon the stage we see him as a kind of beardless youth, or one who has, at all events, the agility and the energy of youth. But I submit that Jack Point is not as young as he would like us to think. Shall I be wrong in suggesting that he is between forty and fifty—an age, that is to say, when the tender passion is not at its strongest ? I have no textual authority for this, but let us take a glimpse at his history, because it may help us better to understand his attitude towards Elsie Maynard.

Jack Point had been at one time the jester to the Archbishop of Canterbury. Now, an Archbishop in the days of old Merrie England was an immensely important person, a great noble whose wealth and prestige were second only, and not a bad second, to those of the King. He had his own court, his own brilliant retinue, and his own palaces. Surely, then, the jester at the archiepiscopal court must have been himself one of the princes of jesters, and

141

his appointment must have been one of the plums of the jesters' profession. Surely, too, it could have been only after he had graduated in the homes of the lower nobility, learnt his business uncommonly well, and had his fame noised abroad that he was invited to " quip you and crank you " in the very court of his Grace the Archbishop. Not even Jack Point—one of the cleverest, most versatile, jesters of his day, as we know—could have obtained that promotion without the passing of years. He was a man of education and culture. He would not have been picked up as a gutter minstrel and installed at once in Lambeth Palace.

Looking back, then, at his history so far as we know it, we find that he had had his long climb up the professional ladder ; that he had become at length the jester to the Archbishop ; that he was so well established in the Archbishop's Court that he could attempt to crack a very personal joke in the ears of the Archbishop ; that this proved to be one personal joke too many ; that he had fallen on evil and penurious times, so protracted, indeed, that he had lost his savings ; that he had descended so far in the social scale that, accomplished humorist though he was, he had to be content to work the round of the village fairs ; that in some unknown circumstances he met Elsie Maynard ; that he probably had to teach her and train her in his repertory of songs and dances, some of them probably done by no one else in the country ; and that together they had " made a poor living." Now, accumulate these details, and you must come to the conclusion, I think, that Jack Point was not at all a young man, and if you want additional evidence, I should say that it is unlikely that a young man would try to find balm for a love trouble in the moralisings of St. Ambrose. Not until middle age would the broken-hearted turn for solace to the Early Fathers !

I suppose the ladies will think what I am going to say is commonplace. The menfolk may think my speculation not uninteresting. We assume that Jack Point was a bachelor. I have doubts about it myself, for it seems inevitable that a man of his nature must have fallen into wedlock, even if he is a widower when we meet him on Tower Green. Still, the book induces us to think of him as a bachelor, and our deductions lead us to think of him as between forty and fifty. And a more exasperating creature, matrimonially considered, than the bachelor in the forties I simply don't know. You can lead him to the nuptial waters, but you cannot make him drink. I suppose it is a fact that, while the young man in the twenties jumps into marriage light-heartedly, taking a chance about what may befall him, and usually coming up top, the older bachelor is a prey to doubts and perplexities, always weighing the pros and cons, and always terribly diffident about taking the plunge.

We see this in actual life again and again. In saying this I do not want to be thought a cynic on marriage. Nor is the old bachelor a cynic.

Although as a rule he is settled in habits, and dislikes the prospect of change solely as change, he does crave understanding companionship. The trouble is that he sees all angles too clearly and wants to balance matters too nicely. He cannot make up his mind, he is fearful about committing himself to indissoluble bonds, he sees the variation between his mental ideal and the physical reality, and it is left to the young lady in the case to make up his mind for him, which she usually does.

Now, I submit that Jack Point had passed the romantic age of youth, and that he was suffering from these procrastinating feelings about Elsie Maynard. She may not have been quite the kind of wife he wanted. Above all else he was an artist in love with his art. My own idea is that, when he said he consented to the mock marriage, it was not because the payment of one hundred crowns soothed the unromantic bargain made at the expense of his sweetheart, but because it would compensate in some measure his professional loss in her as a partner. I think, too, we must remember that he was a man of ambition, so much so that he may have wondered whether, if he retrieved his fortunes at last, this dancing girl would prove equal to his regained social position. Clearly, she was a good colleague at the fairs, but she might have made, intellectually speaking, a precious poor help-mate. Only with these thoughts in his mind could he ever have made himself faithless to the truth proclaimed in one of the operas :

THOUGHTS ABOUT JACK POINT

" Oh, many a man, in friendship's name,
  Has yielded fortune, rank and fame !
  But no one yet, in the world so wide,
  Has yielded up a promised bride."

Considering how dumb and wanting in definite views of her own she is when the Lieutenant makes his proposal about marriage to a condemned man, and also considering how easily she is " swung off her feet " later on by the blandishments of Colonel Fairfax, I personally do think that Elsie Maynard is a trifle " empty-headed." She may have been tired of over-long waiting for Jack Point. She may not have had the pluck to hustle him out of his rooted bachelor ways. In any case she found herself in an unpleasant dilemma, married too hastily to a man she had never seen, and conscious, like many of her sisters who rush to the altar, that she had made a sorry mess of things. She had not much option about jilting him anyhow. What I do object to is the apparent callousness of the manner of her jilting of an old pal who is down on his luck. Even a " little pale fool," as Phœbe describes her, though the words are uttered in jealousy, should not be so dead to the virtues of gratitude and charity.

Jack Point's end has touches of greatness. Not for him the tearing of a passion to tatters or the shrieking of vengeance on the usurper. Not for him any melodramatic " Far, far better thing I do than I have ever done." That would not have been English. And Jack Point, if he was anything, was an Englishman. If fate has turned scurvy, then he will face it calmly, manfully, grimly. Poor fellow ! He has no quips and cranks to suit this tragic business. The glibness of tongue has disappeared. Simply and reverently he kisses the hem of the garment of the girl he has loved and with whom he had shared those vagabond hardships. He is too great-souled to cast the shadow of his own remorse across her happiness. And when he falls, the only tragic figure amidst that merry throng, there is no glance of compassion for a poor fool, no hand stretched out in comfort, no tender word even from the girl whom he had befriended and loved. If Jack Point does die of a broken heart—and it touches the chords of gentle melancholy for us to believe so—then let his simple epitaph be " An Englishman."

CHAPTER XVI

WAYWARD ELSIE MAYNARD

GILBERT'S most interesting couple are certainly Jack Point and Elsie Maynard. They are his most interesting couple but by no means his greatest. They appeal because a tragic strand that divides their lives invites from us " the passing tribute of a sigh." As characters they may leave something wanting. By this I mean that Gilbert is not so sure a character-drawer here as he is elsewhere. He does not seem clear in his own mind and his workmanship in some details is " sketchy."

Jack Point never appeals to me as a great character, judging him strictly by dramatic values, and not by what may constitute a favourite or popular part. The story of the tragic jester, of the breaking heart under the motley, has been done to death by playwrights and novelists, and Gilbert's variation merely translates the old Punchinello idea into the romantic setting of Merrie England. " The Yeomen of the Guard " is remarkable in the sense that its wit and its music, its sentiment and its atmosphere, as we have said before, is essentially English. It is well, nevertheless, not to over-rate that which rings the changes, however ingenuously, on a well-worn subject.

Elsie Maynard is certainly not a well-drawn part. She seems fickle, ungrateful and wayward, though actually this may be accusing her falsely. Gilbert, as I have suggested earlier, was an indifferent hand with his women characters. It is seldom that his women are more than dolls with nice voices. With Elsie the trouble is that the action of the play moves so swiftly that the character cannot be developed properly. The development is not natural or easy. In the course of Act II, for instance, we see this girl in tears, because she finds herself in a terrible mess ; we see her swept off her feet by the swaggering wooing of Colonel Fairfax ; and we see her doting in Colonel Fairfax's arms as if nothing had happened and no one else matters, least of all Point. This, you must agree, is going the pace, even in opera. Gilbert, clearly, was suffering from want of elbow-room, and from the inelasticity of a plot which would not allow him to spread these emotional gymnastics over both acts of the play.

Then it is a baffling matter to probe the exact relationship between Jack Point and Elsie Maynard. Were they sweethearts, or an engaged couple, or just professional partners ? We are clear about the relationship between Strephon and Phyllis. We have a shrewd notion that, despite an unpromising beginning, Robin Oakapple will marry Rose Maybud. Gilbert never intended that Jack and Elsie should marry, at least not during the course of the opera, though he may have conveyed a hint that all would come right long after we, the audience, have bade them good-bye. Gilbert's aim, meanwhile, is to wring our hearts with a sad little drama. Was Jack Point intended to be a jilted lover, or was he meant to have only a sub-conscious fondness for the girl, a dormant emotion that became active only under the stimulus of rivalry ? I am not sure that his creator had clear ideas on the matter himself. The evidence of the libretto is muddled. I fancy that most people who see the opera do accept the two strolling players as lovers, but if one looks into the matter, one finds that few more formal lovers ever stepped on to the stage.

Now, in attempting to get to the bottom of this question, one has to resort to some speculation. Failing any definite guidance, one can draw one's deductions only from what one finds in the text, from various accepted gestures in interpretation. and from what one may assume from a knowledge of human nature. Even then the clues are loose. Search the text, and one discovers that not one word about Jack Point, not one profession either of love or dislike, escapes the lips of Elsie Maynard. A girl of her nature might have been expected to give the key to the mystery. Jack Point is more open. He tells us that :

> " Though as a general rule of life
> I don't allow my promised wife,
> My lovely bride that is to be,
> To marry anyone but me "

—still . . . well, a bargain's a bargain, he virtually says, and if the jingle of the coin is hearty enough, general rules of life may go for once to the dogs. Of course, Jack Point's *obiter dicta* may have reference to any prospective wife, with no special application to Elsie Maynard. But a little later he puts things more concretely. Elsie has undergone her mock marriage, and it transpires that her bridegroom, who was to have been beheaded and conveniently left her a widow within the space of a few hours, has escaped from his jailors. The jester is mournful. "My laugh is dead," he exclaims, "my heart unmanned ; a jester with a heart of lead, a lover loverless I stand." In the circumstances his anguish must be associated with the strange dilemma of Elsie Maynard.

Jack Point, one has a suspicion, was a cynic on marriage. "Are ye man and wife ? " asks the Lieutenant. "No, sir," quickly comes the reply, "for though I'm a fool there is a limit to my folly." I agree that we should not take this saying too seriously. In any case a jester had to be funny. But at all events it does not support the view that Jack Point was intensely anxious to marry Elsie Maynard. And what about another of his sayings ? "Men and women," he exclaims, "marry every day with none to say ' Oh ! the pity of it ! ' but I and fools like me." These are not the words of a marrying man, nor is the sentiment a tactful one, to say the least of it, to express in the presence of the lady of one's choice. I warrant that Giuseppe never dare have uttered words like these in the hearing of a pert maiden like Tessa.

Elsie's silence amid this shower of epigrams is a little confusing. She may, long-suffering soul, have heard them often and often. And she was not quick-witted enough to cap them with better epigrams. If only this reticent girl were more talkative, if only she had more sparkle and self-assertion, we should be less in the dark about her feelings towards the jester. You will remember the incident where Jack Point exclaims " For though I am not wedded to Elsie Maynard, time works wonders, and there's no knowing what may be in store for us." Here at least is a moment when a girl with a mind of her own would have something to say. She might be faithful to the traditions of her sex and deny it flatly. She might, if she were more honest, look charmingly winsome and coy.

Some interpreters of the part, I believe, give an involuntary start when these words are spoken, as much as to imply " What is he saying ? Is he in earnest ? " If this is, as I have been told, the authentic form of interpretation, then it suggests that she did want to marry him, and that this was the first she had heard that he returned her affection. If, on the other hand, we accept the presumption that they were engaged, then obviously this theory falls to the ground. What I should like to know is : what wonders were there that time had to work ? What was the hindrance to marriage ? It would be the modest marriage of a couple who were tramping the country and could just make a poor living. They would have made ends meet better as man and wife than independently. Was Jack Point or Elsie Maynard the obstinate party ?

In the preceding chapter I have surmised that the jester had doubts whether the girl, although a good partner, would 'be a good help-mate. He may have felt that she was his for the asking and there was no need to hurry. Here I would canvass a different view. It is the view that Point *was* in earnest, and that he wanted to marry Elsie, whatever jibes about matrimony he might retail for the " gallery." She in her turn could not make up her mind—and he was not the type of man to apply the amatory coaxing. We have it on record that he knew not how to woo a fair maid. When he believed that she was free of Fairfax, he tried to commend himself to her anew by saying that he had a pretty wit, and that he could " jest you, jibe you, quip you, crank you." That was his notion of love-making. " Tush, man," interrupts Fairfax, " thou knowest not how to woo. 'Tis not done with time-worn jests and thread-bare sophistries : with quips, conundrums, rhymes and paradoxes. 'Tis an art in itself and must be studied gravely and conscientiously." It had indeed ! Jack Point realised this too late when, with honeyed words and tender embraces, the artful fellow dazzled and won the impressionable girl under his very eyes. Poor Jack Point ! He could love but he could not woo. In real life he has many brothers.

152

And yet I fancy few are such clumsy tacticians in the tender art as to leave their wooing to be done for them by proxy.

Let us be fair to Elsie. She must have been bored to death by those stale jokes and threadbare sophistries. She had borne them when they were entertaining the crowds, and she had to endure them when the fool was pressing his suit, and when once again all his stock-in-trade was displayed. Point was fond of art for art's sake and his work was his passion. Elsie, for all we know, hated the vagabond life, and she was hardly to be won by this talking of " shop." She " loves brave men," she tells us, and Jack Point would have realised the right line of attack had he seriously turned his mind to love-making and " studied all day in methodical way." She was the romantic type of girl who would be swept off her feet more easily by a soldier's red coat than a clown's motley.

And in any case there is nothing very heroic about the jester.[1] We see that soon after his first entry. Elsie is jostled by the crowd and one unmannerly fellow handles her roughly. Jack Point does not rush to her side as her protector and companion. He has come to the Tower to entertain, and if he gets mixed up in a brawl, it will do business no good. So he accepts discretion as the better part of valour, and takes refuge in some of those inevitable, irrepressible jokes. Later Elsie, assailed

[1] See article by R. G. Davis, *Gilbert and Sullivan Journal*, April 1926.

in the same unwelcome fashion, draws her dagger in her own protection. " This is going too far " interposes the jester, conciliatorily certainly, but just as certainly not courageously. Such a mild exclamation is worthy neither of a chivalrous man nor of a colleague. A worse instance still of his cowardice comes at the close of the first act of the opera. The crowd have scattered in alarm. And Jack Point slinks off with them. He may have gone in search of the fugitive who has escaped from the dungeon. But his place, whether as lover or as companion, is surely by the side of Elsie Maynard. She has swooned, and she is left in the arms of that ominous stranger, Colonel Fairfax.

Elsie found her brave man. But did she live to rue it ? Did she learn that a dashing wooer may prove sometimes an inconstant mate ? Did she realise, this proud but humble maid, that marriage into a great family was a boon that could be bought at too hard a price ? I suggest that Elsie's bliss as we see it when the curtain falls is a mirage. The dream was soon to be over. For my evidence I ask you to turn to the prophetic thread which is woven, and very deftly woven, into the Merryman's song. Now, in the earlier verses, we identify the moping Merryman with Jack Point himself, and we identify the Merrymaid with Elsie Maynard. The singers may be unconscious of it, but they foreshadow what is going to happen to them, and not to some entirely legendary couple. And why should the last verse be anything less of an allegory ? It refers to events which occur, if they occur at all, after the close of the opera. It suggests that another chapter ought to be written, and that that chapter would show that there was a touching sequel, after all, to the jester's tragedy. Study well this final verse :

> " I have a song to sing, O !
>   Sing me your song, O !
>   It is sung with a sigh
>   And a tear in the eye
>   For it tells of a righted wrong, O !
> It's a song of a merrymaid, once so gay,
> Who turned on her heel and tripped away
> From the peacock popinjay, bravely born,
> Who turned up his noble nose with scorn
> At the humble heart that he did not prize :
> So she begged on her knees, with downcast eyes,
> For the love of the merryman, moping mum,
> Whose soul was sad and whose glance was glum,
> Who sipped no cup, and who craved no crumb,
>   As he sighed for the love of a ladye !
>   Heighdy ! heighdy !
>   Misery me, lackadaydee,
>   His pains were o'er, and he sighed no more,
>   For he lived in the love of a ladye ! "

Clearly, the " peacock popinjay " can be no other than Colonel Fairfax, perhaps a man who would be all too conscious, in the days of his freedom, that he owned " the handsomest head in England." That he was bravely born, that he was a valiant soldier and an ardent lover, we know from the story. By what line of argument can you resist my theory that, having won the humble heart of Elsie Maynard in the strange adventure on Tower Green, he became fickle and indifferent towards one drawn from a lower station in life, and that the disillusioned girl went back to Jack Point to claim from him anew the solace and devotion of their lowly vagabond days ? That, I submit, is the sequel which we must infer from thé song, and it is a sequel which suggests that there was a happier ending to their companionship than the one we see on the stage. In other words, the lovers were re-united, and the jester found at last that " naught was truer than his joy."

I know that this surmise, if surmise it is, disturbs one convention about " The Yeomen of the Guard." Jack Point did not die ! True it is, indeed, that in the text we are simply told that he falls insensible when he finds his little world loveless and empty, but it has long been accepted that his great heart was broken by the intensity of his tragedy. Gilbert had too sure a dramatic touch to mar the poignancy of this closing setting. Earlier on, nevertheless, he had lifted the veil on the future, and from this we may believe, or believe if we will, that the wrong done to the jester was to be righted, and that after all the sighing and pursuing, honest Jack Point did at last " *live* in the love of a ladye."

CHAPTER XVII

THE ROYAL SEVEN

GILBERT was frankly iconoclastic in his treatment of Royalty. You will remember that cruel burlesque of a Court function in " Utopia." When King Paramount and his officers of State sat round in Christy minstrel fashion, there was never any doubt that it was a satire, and a deliberate one, on a Drawing-room at St. James's. It was regarded as so offensive that, according to popular report, no member of the real Court would see the opera a second time at the Savoy. This does not imply that it oversteps the bounds of taste to-day. The times have changed, and they have brought with them a heartier, more tolerant outlook. The French are less incensed about a certain uncomplimentary ballad in " Ruddigore." Our old friend " The Mikado " is no longer banned lest conceivably it should offend international scruples.[1] The world has taken on a broader sanity.

[1] It was in 1907 that the Lord Chamberlain imposed his ban on this opera, and according to Gilbert, who was most indignant, it was done at the instigation of the Japanese and in order that " offence " might not be done to Prince Fushimi, who was coming to England. Questions were raised in the House of Commons and scathing articles appeared in the newspapers. The ban was removed the following year.

When I described the " Utopia " burlesque as cruel I was thinking of the times in which the opera was written. They were serious people in those days. The Court itself was solemn, and it was outrageous that a popular dramatist, one who had had a fair share of its favours, should give its austere leg a by no means gentle pulling. Gilbert, however, seemed to have taken the line that, if an institution is healthily rooted, ridicule will pour off it as easily as water off a duck's back, and he was trespassing merely upon what he knew was the downright soundness of the British people regarding the Monarchy. Not that this was his first lapse from politeness. In " The Gondoliers " there is a quartet which, if one is thin-skinned, may seem to be wanting a little in loyal respect. In a way it is more daring, inasmuch as it was more pointedly personal, than the burlesque in " Utopia." Still, the best answer to this objection is that, when Queen Victoria emerged at last from the long retirement after the Prince Consort's death, the play selected for the first Command Performance at Windsor Castle was " The Gondoliers." The Royal programme omitted the dramatist's name, attributing the work to the composer alone, though it transpired that this was an unfortunate oversight only.

Four kings, one reigning prince, and two reigning dukes appear in the operas. Seeing that a Ruritanian princeling finds his way into every other musical comedy, the writers of which seem to be unable to get on without him, this number is not at all generous. The Royal seven that Gilbert drew, however, are all interesting as character sketches, no less so because they do not conform to one common pattern. Some of them wear the purple lightly, and some would find existence less irksome, one gathers, but for the chronic emptiness of their exchequers. Only two of them could gamble on an unshakeable tenure of their thrones. One of these is the Mikado—one includes him in the kingly category for the sake of convenience— and the other is Hildebrand. Of this latter Monarch I have not much to say. " Princess Ida " tells us little about his record or his character, and if we must generalise from what we do know of him, then we may suspect that he is a tyrant. He himself declares that he is a peppery kind of king who is not disposed for parleying. Least of all is he inclined for it—and here we have a nimble Gilbert line— " to fit the wit of a bit of a chit." Hildebrand appears before us as a tall, upstanding figure who wears his coat of mail with an air, and who labours under none of the eccentricities of operatic kings and prince-lings. He comes nearest to the accepted standards of kingship. He seems " out of his beat " in Gilbert and Sullivan.

The Mikado came to the Throne as a reforming zealot and a model philanthropist. He has a brain that teems with ideas. The first crusade on which he entered was that to curb the Don Juans among the young bloods of Japan. The " youth who winked a roving eye or breathed a non-connubial sigh " was forthwith to be beheaded. So anti-romantic an edict would have decapitated half the unwedded population. From the evidence of the opera—in which there are flirtatious incidents not a few—it must have broken down already. In his determination to make the punishment fit the crime this ingenious ruler was on more plausible ground. The Imperial ardour to cleanse the land of dull society sinners and amateur tenors may strike some of us, judged solely as an ideal, and without regard to the means to attain that ideal, as the acme of enlightenment.

Nanki-Poo describes his father as the " Lucius Junius Brutus of his race." He had ordered the son to marry an elderly lady of the court or perish on the scaffold. Lucius Junius Brutus was the Roman consul, the famous " avenger of woman's honour," to whose memory the Roman matrons erected a statue on the Capitol. When his two sons were found to be implicated in a conspiracy to overthrow the dynasty, not only did he himself sentence them to death, but they were executed in his own presence.[1] And the Mikado would have been Spartan enough to watch the knife fall on the neck of Nanki-Poo. It may even be doubted whether an ordinary execution would have been sufficiently grim for his liking. For this Mikado has a marvellously inventive mind in the matter of excruciating punishments. Witness the enumeration of horror

[1] It is worth mentioning that this conspiracy of the two sons was the subject of a tragedy by Voltaire.

on horror in the last verse of his grisly-humorous song. The Mikado must have been an enthusiastic cue-ist himself. By what other means may we account for the heaping on a common billiard sharp of such a catalogue of hallucinations and agonies? Even an Edgar Allan Poe could not have described in sufficiently vivid prose the delirium of this victim of an Oriental despot in the fulfilment of an object all sublime:

> " The billiard sharp whom any one catches
>   His doom's extremely hard :
>   He's made to dwell
>   In a dungeon cell
>   On a spot that's always barred ;
> And there he plays extravagant matches
>   In fitless finger stalls,
>   On a cloth untrue
>   With a twisted cue
>   And elliptical billiard-balls."

And yet it is not as the scourger of wrongs that the fame of this great man is going down to posterity. It was the cause of " innocent merriment " of his subjects that first and foremost set his mind working away from the ordinary grooves. At one and the same time, according to his code of justice, the evil liver was to suffer for his sins, and the public was to see how unerringly and how wittily the punishment fitted. There was logic in that. And the Mikado is essentially a logical person. Witness, for instance, his discovery that there is no difference between the judge who condemned a criminal to die and the industrious mechanic who carried out the sentence, and his decree that the two offices should thenceforward be rolled into one. The Mikado, to be sure, has some lovable traits. Could there be anything nicer than his invitation to the functionaries who have beheaded his son to take tea with him before their shrieks in the boiling oil cause his benevolent heart to throb with delight ? You may think it is harsh and inconsistent. It is nothing of the kind. Ko-Ko, Pooh-Bah and Petty-Sing may have to have a bad time, but what is that compared with the delicious fund of merriment that their lingering agonies will yield to this fatherly potentate's subjects ? And why not some kindly pleasantries beforehand with those whimsical martyrs who have to be butchered and boiled to make an Oriental holiday ?

It is not the Mikado alone whose laudable mission it is to minister to the gaiety of the populace. King Paramount—and apparently these two men were contemporary rulers [1]—is in the same position. It may be true that in his case the rôle is less sublime because it was not of his choosing. He is an absolute Monarch theoretically only, because he is the chief figure in that novel constitutional experiment, a " despotism tempered by dynamite." So long as he behaves himself all may be well, but a vigilant watch is kept on His Majesty's illicities,

[1] " I am waiting," says King Paramount, " until a punishment is discovered that will exactly meet the enormity of the case. I am in constant communication with the Mikado of Japan, who is a leading authority on such points."

and a Public Exploder has to be ready on good cause being shown to explode a " pound of dynamite in his articulars." Even the sportive ruler from Tokio never invented a diversion half as charming as Scaphio and Phantis do in " Utopia." A bizarre couple they are with a vengeance. They command Paramount to concoct spicy scandals about himself for the columns of the " Palace Peeper." All his " goings on " have to be chronicled with vivid embellishments in that outrageous organ. They also compel him to write an opera, with himself the object of caricature, entitled " King Tuppence." King Paramount, to give him his due, sees the joke of the thing. Note his chuckle when he recalls the " stinging little paragraphs " of which he is both victim and author, and especially when he points with paternal pride to droll features like " Another Royal Scandal " by Junius Junior ; " How long is this to last ? " by Senex Senior ; " Ribald Royalty " by Mercury Major ! With truth he confesses that this showing up of his Royal indiscretions to order is one of the funniest things within his experience. I agree that it is one of the brightest ideas to be found in the operas.

King Paramount is without a doubt a fine fellow. Spineless he may be—at least until he sees that the hour is safe for revolt—but no one ever wore his fetters and suffered indignities with such unaffected good spirits. A jollier crowned head never reigned —on the stage. Compare him but for a moment with his brother Gama. Paramount is all sly winks

and fantastic capers. Gama excels only in his gift
of biting epigram. He has an irritating chuckle,
a celebrated sneer, an entertaining snigger, and a
fascinating leer. He is a meddlesome old busy-body
who finds the day flat and wearisome if it hasn't a
grumble. The captive hunchback makes a good
dramatic part. Gilbert has only two other male
characters that call for the same skilful acting. But
here we are examining his conceptions of kingship,
and we must concede that his monarch in " Princess
Ida " is of hard, ungracious mettle in contrast with
the benevolent autocrat who enlivens " The Mikado "
and the cheery despot under control who prances
gaily through " Utopia Limited."

And now we come to the dukes. The Duke of
Plaza-Toro makes his bow before us in the habili-
ments of shabby gentility. I hope I shall not be
thought captious in saying that to me this is unconvincing. Neither the Duchess nor Casilda is
dressed at all badly. The " suite," if small in
number, makes up for it in sartorial quality, and it is
odd that ducal economies have not permitted the
well-connected nobleman himself to replace his
dinted breast-plate. The Duke, who is a Castilian
and a member of a proud race, admits quite frankly
that he never had any stomach for fighting. In
time of war *his* object all sublime was to " preserve
his gore O ! " It was his habit to lead his regiment
from behind because he found it less exciting. It
is not surprising that, with such a leader, the regiment lost its morale, played the coward, and went

into hiding. It seems to have been rather a discreditable page in military history. And yet this Duke could be a prompt man of action in some things.

> " When told that they would all be shot
>   Unless they left the service,
> That hero hesitated not,
>   So marvellous his nerve is.
> He sent his resignation in,
>   The first of all his corps, O !
>   That very knowing,
>   Overflowing,
>   Easy-going
>   Paladin,
> The Duke of Plaza-Toro ! "

But, in any case, how came his Grace to be poor ? He is a man of infinite resource. He has schemes without end for turning in money. He is not averse to a little artful commercialisation of his position. Small titles and orders obtained for mayors and recorders are presumably acknowledged handsomely. Foundation-stone laying he finds very paying. At charity dinners, the best of speech-spinners, he gets ten per cent. on the takings. He has a hand in company bubbles, and as soon as they are floated, he is freely bank-noted, and pretty well paid for his trouble. And so on. Such ever-ready adaptability should have been lucrative enough for the wildest of spendthrifts. Nor can one overlook his boldest business stroke, that of getting himself issued as a public company, and going to allotment at a big premium. This last expedient was resorted to in order to raise the funds for his daughter's marriage. Later in " The Gondoliers " we see him adorned with silks and periwigs and attended by retainers. It is presumptive evidence that some part of his unaccustomed pocket-money had been diverted from its intended purpose. And why not ? As King Luiz's father-in-law he will have profitable social " opportunities " that will leave in the shade all those he has had as an industrious grandee of Spain.

If no man is a hero to his valet, how much worse is the case of Rudolph, Grand Duke of Pfennig-Halbpfennig ? In the eyes of his troop of chamberlains he is a miserable prig. And most certainly their estimate is just. He is a miser and spineless. He maintains an insufferable ducal pomp while he goes about with his elbows patched. He keeps a retinue to bow and scrape to him while he ponders whether for once he should indulge in an egg for his breakfast. He is so miserly that a jujube is put by for his supper. He is a dull and wearisome creature—as dull and wearisome as the opera in which he appears.

Strangely or otherwise, both Gilbert's dukes are down at heels when we meet them, and this is not the sum total of their similarity. Rudolph, like Plaza-Toro, has notions of his own about raising the cash, and one of his schemes is that all courting, including his own, shall be done publicly in the Market Place. The reason for this is that there is a Royal monopoly in the sale of opera-glasses, and that it makes desirable residential properties of decayed houses that have, for instance, drains dating back to the days of Charlemagne. Spain's well-connected, unaffected son is not an autocrat who could stoop to this kind of trick, but rather a hail-fellow-well-met man of the people. When he wants to finance a wedding he boldly and triumphantly turns himself into a company. The Grand Duke Rudolph faces the dilemma in a different way when he is about to become a bride-groom. The wedding is to be "the first little treat he has allowed himself since his christening." He commands the inhabitants to send him magni-ficent presents, to do their own illuminating and entertaining, and to purchase at the usual discount prices copies of a special anthem he has composed. Actually that ceremony never takes place. But the romantic misadventures of this sorry mortal are not worth following up. He is a poor specimen as a man and worse than that as a stage puppet.

The Prince of Monte Carlo—why was this title chosen?—is also introduced to us in "The Grand Duke." If he had been introduced earlier, and not at the very end, it might have been a much brighter opera. The Prince seems to be a near relative of the amiable Plaza-Toro. Like him, he has a charming daughter betrothed in infancy, and it is for her marriage that he has brought her over the seas to the Grand Duchy. Like Plaza-Toro also, he is an impecunious fellow, though he takes more care in concealing the fact. For his retinue he has employed six theatre supernumeraries—his useful working set of second-hand nobles—at a wage of one-and-sixpence a day. They are illiterate, they wear their liveries awkwardly, they have to be instructed in the arts of deportment, and their nails are so unpresentable that they cannot remove their gloves. The Prince is also attended by a costumier. At home, as he confesses frankly, his own clothes " are much gloomier."

Gilbert carries forward the parallel. The Duke of Plaza-Toro obtains funds by placing himself on the Stock Exchange. The Prince also makes money. And, to give him his due, he made it before he set out with his daughter. During his enforced leisure in his palace, to which he was confined to avoid a warrant for his arrest, he had been studying the doctrine of chance, and " this led to the discovery of a singularly fascinating little round game which I have called roulette." And at a single sitting he won three thousand francs, and regained his credit and his liberty. The Prince is an engaging character after the Grand Duke Rudolph. He, at least, is neither a miser nor a prig, tolerant though he be towards that " enthusiastic collector of coins of the realm," and willing though he is to make allowances for " a numismatist if he feels a certain disinclination to part with some of his really very valuable specimens."

Up till now I have omitted a reference to one other King—a King in the dual personality of our old friends Marco and Giuseppe. They, after all, were kings only for a fleeting, rollicking spell, and were neither born in nor meant for the purple. They were honest gondoliers, who revelled like schoolboys in a novel adventure, but who were glad enough to take off their crowns and their robes and get back to their ordinary calling. The feature of their reign was the re-modelling of the monarchy on republican principles. Short-lived though their dynasty was, it had incident enough and to spare, and probably under the direction of good wives they would have had more common sense than all the others who wielded the Gilbertian sceptre. At all events they deserve admission to an illustrious gallery.

CHAPTER XVIII

SELF-MADE MEN

In real life a self-made man is not always a likeable person. The grimness of the battle is on him, and his personality has often the abrupt, unyielding hardness of granite. He is seldom a believer in luck. Success, as he sees it, comes only to the swift and the strong. He has been the architect of his own fortunes, a model to the world of the rewards of shrewdness, integrity and enterprise. In the popular periodicals he may condescend to tell us " How I began." It is the first chapter in an epic of self-glorification. Seldom does he own anything to happy chance, to the trimming of his sails to the favouring breezes, or to the loyalty of his subordinates. The type is sometimes self-opinionated and pompous.

Now, Gilbert has a fondness for the self-made man, and his treatment of him makes an interesting study. At least three of his leading characters belong to the species. They are the Judge in " Trial by Jury," Sir Joseph Porter in " H.M.S. Pinafore," and Ko-Ko in " The Mikado." And the three of them have an engaging similarity.

Two of them are lawyers. The third is—or was, before we meet him—a tailor. This fact is in itself worth notice. For Gilbert has no time for tradesmen. He is tolerant towards parsons, policemen and pirates, but the honest man who serves behind the counter is disdained and ignored. Perhaps it *is* difficult to make a romantic operatic figure out of a grocer. At all events I recall only one representative of the tradesman class in the dramatist's gallery. He is a dealer in magic and spells, and a crude, unmannerly creature in a ludicrous garb. You will not overlook that a melodramatic descent into the infernal regions is the end of this John Wellington Wells. In the old days a man who soiled his fingers in trade was no fit associate for the quality. In a different form the prejudice survived in the popular caricatures of war profiteers. Gilbert seems to have been true to the caste traditions of his own and succeeding ages.

But let us return to the matter at issue. The Judge, Sir Joseph Porter and Ko-Ko have each been wafted from obscurity into wealth and position. The heights to which two of them scaled must have been blinding. The ordinary parvenu would have lost his head completely. In his less intoxicated moments he would blow boastful blasts on the trumpet. And in course of time he would become dyspeptic or haughty. But with these three worthies it is a different tale altogether. They treat the whole thing as a wonderful joke. A

Victorian statesman once said that there was " no damned merit " about the conferment of the Order of the Garter. And none of these three claims that there was any merit about his own rise from lowly beginnings. In one case it was due to unblushing trickiness and jobbery. In another case it was due to dutiful attention to detail. And in the third a set of curious chances translated a jail-bird into a chief officer of State.

In their different ways a jollier trio never set foot on the stage. In my view the Judge is the merriest fellow in Gilbert and Sullivan. The frankness of the fellow is brazen. The court have swung their censers of adulation and homage. In return he offers to tell them—and they repeat his words with bated breath—how he rose to his judgeship. The stage is set for an outburst of autobiographical glorification. " Swank," however, is not one of the attributes, not even in the mildest form, of this extraordinary Judge. Like certain men of nobler breeding, he makes no pretence to intellectual eminence or scholarship sublime, and what little law he knows, he openly confesses, is fudge. There had been a time when, as a briefless barrister, he had danced " like a semi-despondent fury." Some short cut to affluence had to be found, and he discovered one by offering to marry a rich attorney's elderly, ugly daughter. And then, when the briefs came trooping gaily, and with them reputation and riches, he blandly threw over the unattractive spinster. And with this avowal of his own romantic perfidy the cynic announces his readiness to try the present breach of promise of marriage. It is all very outrageous and topsy-turvy.

Sir Joseph Porter [1] is a shining example of the success of the industrious apprentice. Here again there is no nonsense about merit as the foundation of fortune. He got on in business because he polished up the door handle, served the writs with a smile so bland, and wore clean collars and a brand new suit. Later, when he became rich and entered Parliament, it was not his gifts as a spokesman, but his unfailing talent as a good party hack, that carried him, a land-lubber, to the Admiralty. Confessions of this nature are tactless. It is not fashionable for a successful man of business to declare that he was once merely a dutiful clerk. Nor does a Cabinet Minister ever split his sides when telling his doting relatives that a greater ignoramus never took office. It is not done. Sir Joseph's frankness is fatal to the tradition that in such circumstances one should maintain a proud upper lip.

One curious point we may note in passing. The First Lord is a bachelor. Considering what an eligible party he is, one can only wonder why his swarm of sisters, cousins and aunts have allowed him to escape the matrimonial fetters so long. Certainly Hebe, his first cousin, captures him

[1] Shortly before *H.M.S. Pinafore* was produced, Mr. W. H. Smith, of bookstall fame, had become Disraeli's First Lord of the Admiralty. Like Sir Joseph Porter, whose model he was in this respect, and in this one respect only, he had " never been to sea." Smith was ever afterwards nicknamed " Pinafore Smith."

without much trouble when he has been rejected by Josephine. The Judge is also a bachelor. In the course of the breach of promise case this outrageous philanderer openly flirts with one of the bridesmaids and with the plaintiff. And in the end, as the easiest means of solving a tangle, he offers to marry the jilted maiden himself. Nearly all the leading humorous characters, the youngest and the oldest of them, are bachelors when we first meet them, though they do not seem to be the type of men who would ordinarily avoid the ranks of the " conjugally matrimonified." [1] The great exception is the Duke of Plaza-Toro. He is a husband, and a hen-pecked husband, one shrewdly suspects, into the bargain.

Ko-Ko, who is one of the bachelors, began life as a cheap tailor in Titipu. He was sentenced to death for flirting. The convict is reprieved, and soon finds himself, not wielding the scissors again, but bearing the ceremonial axe of the Lord High Executioner and holding one of the most exalted ranks in Japan. Ko-Ko's keen sense of humour is his salvation. He is a Jack-in-office, probably unlettered and untaught, who refuses to be over-whelmed by his advancement, and who tumbles into scrapes and out of them with the zest of a schoolboy. " Gentlemen," he tells the courtiers, " I am much touched by this reception. I can only trust that by strict attention to duty I shall ensure

[1] This term is used with due acknowledgments to the Penzance Pirates.

a continuation of those favours which it will ever be my study to deserve." It sounds like an extract from a tradesman's circular touting for orders for ready-made garments. In all probability it is a form of acknowledgment which he has committed to memory and recites at every function because of his inability to make an extemporary speech.

Only in Gilbertania, of course, would a humane little creature like Ko-Ko, who has not the heart to wring even a bluebottle's neck,[1] obtain appointment to a Lord High Executionership. He has certainly compiled a comprehensive list of society offenders who might well be underground. But, apart from this most admirable schedule, there is little evidence that the novice in office has paid any "strict attention to duty." After a month without an execution a victim has to be found. Seeing that "apologetic statesmen of a compromising kind" are on his list of desirable decapitations, it is a wonder that he does not take his apologetic and compromising friend, the bulky Lord High Everything Else. Ko-Ko is a hearty liar and a man not overburdened with scruples. He adores Yum-Yum, but he admits that he adores himself better, and he is ready enough to surrender her to save his

---

[1] Ko-Ko's declaration that he had "never even killed a bluebottle" recalls a statement of Gilbert about himself. "I don't think I ever killed a black-beetle" said the dramatist once. "The time will come when the sport of the present day will be regarded very much as we regard the Spanish bull-fight or the bear-baiting of our ancestors."

own neck from "the sensation of a short, sharp shock from a cheap and chippy chopper on a big black block." The best there is to be said of this upstart is that he has a sense of humour. It is his sense of humour that enables him to treat Pooh-Bah, a noble whose ancestral pride is something terrific, on easy terms as a familiar, and not to lose his head (in any sense) over the supposed execution of the Heir-Apparent.

Strictly, Ko-Ko is not a self-made man, because he was neither born great nor achieved greatness, but had greatness thrust upon him. But as an example of one of the lower orders lifted above and beyond his normal station he makes an interesting study. Ko-Ko takes us into his confidence from the beginning. He relishes the idea that the favouring gales have wafted him miraculously from prison to pomp. He accepts it as excruciatingly funny. The Judge is also as disconcertingly frank and as incorrigibly merry. So is Sir Joseph Porter, though one detects unction in his manner at times, and he is growing self-conscious in his position.

Gilbert's self-made men may not be true to type. They are not replicas of the real thing but their whimsical opposites. It was a clever stroke of his, a touch of burlesque which, perhaps, escapes us when we are appraising his satirical gift. Gilbert may have known the real self-made man at his worst—that cocksure creature who is always parading his opulence and flaunting his hard-headed sagacity as an example for lesser mortals to copy.

Gilbert just turns the type topsy-turvy. The satire of it all is as adroit as it is delicious.

We observed at the outset that two of these three parvenus were lawyers. By way of addendum to this chapter I may mention that in the full *dramatis personae* of the operas there are eleven representatives of this learned profession. We exclude Pooh-Bah in his sundry legal capacities. Some of them, like the notaries, are merely transient figures, but there are two, Scaphio and Phantis, who are the " villains of the piece." For light operas, which usually specialise in gay figures and dashing uniforms, the lawyers are numerically a strong contingent. They are outnumbered only by the soldiers, of whom there are about a score, apart from the warriors there are amongst the ancestral ghosts of Castle Ruddigore.

In all there are one hundred and sixty-seven specified parts in the Gilbert and Sullivan Opera. " Trial by Jury " has the fewest of them with eight. Strangely enough, " The Mikado " has only nine, though all of them are very definite parts to be taken only by experienced principals. The largest caste is that in " Utopia." It has eighteen characters, or one more than we find in " Ruddigore," " The Gondoliers," or " The Grand Duke." Gilbert was fairly economical with his principal parts. In the case of " The Gondoliers," indeed, he deliberately contrived, so we are told, that there should be no rôle with any undue prominence. In this opera in which " all shall equal be " there was to be equality even amongst his principals. This was because he believed that certain artists thought that they alone were responsible for the success of the operas.[1]   And he was determined " to put a stop to the thing."

[1] This is stated by Miss Jessie Bond, *Strand Magazine*, December 1925.   " We'll have an opera," Gilbert exclaimed, " in which there will be no principal parts.   No character shall stand out more prominently than another."   Soon afterwards (adds Miss Bond) *The Gondoliers* was written, and, strangely enough, it was found to contain no rôle of outstanding importance.

CHAPTER XIX

THE EQUALITY COMEDY

WE shall see later that the Bab Ballads are the leaven
of Gilbert and Sullivan. It is of interest at this
moment to note how similar ideas are re-introduced
in the operas. In some cases it is the same idea,
and in other cases the idea is carried further, given
a more whimsical twist, or possibly turned topsy-
turvy. The " King Charles's Head " in Gilbert's
libretti is that quaint notion about equality. It
occurs again and again, the only difference being
that, whereas in the earlier operas it is usually
social equality, in the later ones it takes a more
political tinge. It was a pretty affectation, and one
which the dramatist could never have believed in
himself, and in the end he explodes it completely.

Speaking for the moment, however, about the
recurrence of ideas in the operas, let us note first of
all the similarity between those two rulers, Gama
and the Mikado. Gama, of course, is a meddlesome misanthropist, but when he tells us that

" Each little fault of temper and each social defect
 In my erring fellow-creatures I endeavour to correct "

we are struck by the parallel case in the immediately succeeding opera of the " virtuous man " who, on ascending the throne of Japan, " resolved to try a plan whereby young men might best be steadied." Flirting was the social defect which this true philanthropist set out first of all to remedy.

Again, when the King of the Penzance Pirates, who holds that, contrasted with respectability, his calling is " comparatively honest," declares that :

> " Many a king on a first-class throne,
> If he wants to call his crown his own,
> Must manage somehow to get through
> More dirty work than ever *I* do "

we have a glimpse of an idea that Gilbert elaborated effectively in the case of Marco and Giuseppe. The " dirty work " which these adaptable rulers have to do takes the literal form of lighting the palace fires and polishing the regalia and the coronation plate.

The Duke of Plaza-Toro, as a means of retrieving his fortunes, floats himself as a limited company. In the succeeding opera an entire population issue themselves individually as joint stock undertakings. Every man, woman and child in Utopia becomes a limited company, with liability restricted to the amount of his or her declared capital. FitzBattleaxe tells us that " there is not a christened baby who has not already issued his little prospectus." The result of the experiment was deplorable.

A curious contrast is that of the Judge and the

Lord Chancellor. The Judge has but a thinly veiled contempt for the dignity of his profession. In his advocate days, and as a means of restoring thieves to " their friends and their relations," he resorted to the bluster of a Serjeant Buzfuz. The Lord Chancellor learnt as a barrister, on the other hand, that it was an unwise maxim to attempt in any way to throw dust in the jurymen's eyes. He decided also—what one may be pretty sure the Judge never did—that :

> " My learned profession I'll never disgrace
>   By taking a fee with a grin on my face."

Sir Joseph Porter propounds the golden rule that success in life is the reward of the man who dutifully sticks to his job. This is the " office desk " policy in its widest application. Everybody will not agree with him in this, and least of all Robin Oakapple, who urges that advancement in life is won by those who " stir it and stump it, and blow their own trumpet." Without one thus acclaims oneself from the housetops one " hasn't a chance." Bunthorne would certainly concur with this statement. He, of all men, knew the showman's arts of self-advertisement, and in a confidential moment he admits that his medievalism is a mere affectation, born of a morbid love of admiration. Ludwig, in " The Grand Duke," rather reminds one of Bunthorne, by the way, when he confides that his " erudition sham is but classical pretention, the result of steady ' cram.' "

Ko-Ko and Jack Point do not seem to be likely subjects of similarity. You will remember, however, that Ko-Ko allows Nanki-Poo to be married to Yum-Yum, his prospective bride, for a month, when Nanki-Poo is to be beheaded and the way left clear again for the Lord High Executioner. Nanki-Poo escapes the block, and so does Colonel Fairfax, who had entered into the same curious arrangement with Jack Point regarding Elsie Maynard. Ko-Ko took a gamble with chance to extricate himself from an awkward official predicament. The little Jack-in-office shed no tears when his fiancée failed to become a widow according to plan. He contracted another marriage, and it was a marriage that would associate him, an ex-tailor jailbird, with the Imperial House of Japan. With Jack Point the fates decreed very differently.

In " The Grand Duke " Rudolph has something to say about the cost of his nuptial celebrations being borne by the public purse. It recalls a similar discussion between Pooh-Bah and Ko-Ko. In " The Grand Duke " also there is an incident that might have been elaborated from " Utopia." The ladies who attend the Drawing-room hand their cards to the Groom-in-Waiting, who passes them to the Lord-in-Waiting, who passes them to the Vice-Chamberlain, who passes them to the Lord Chamberlain, who reads the names to the King. The display of sycophancy is very laughable. In " The Grand Duke " the seven Chamberlains stand in a row, and there is much affected ceremonial when, first a snuff-box, and then a handkerchief, is passed along the line, from the junior of them to the senior, until the article reaches Rudolph. Later on the idea is played with in the dialogue :

> " GRAND DUKE (to Ludwig) : Who are you who presume to address me in person ? If you've anything to communicate, you must fling yourself at the feet of my Acting Temporary Sub-Deputy Assistant Vice-Chamberlain, who will fling himself at the feet of his immediate superior, and so on, with successive foot-flingings through the various grades ; your communication will, in course of time, come to my august knowledge."

Gilbert is fond of a mix-up of identities in babyhood. This had occurred in the case of Corcoran and Rackstraw, and it had occurred also in the case of Luiz, Marco and Giuseppe. He is also partial to infant engagements and marriages. It was as an infant that the Prince of Monte Carlo's daughter was engaged to the Grand Duke Rudolph. Casilda and Luiz were in their cradles when they were married by proxy. Princess Ida and Prince Hilarion were also probably married when they were in the nursery. The textual evidence on this matter is not clear. There are references both to a betrothal and to a marriage twenty years previously, and the more concise of these references do, indeed, point to a marriage. In Tennyson's poem, it is true, there are no indications of these babyhood nuptials, but this would be only one of many licences the play takes with the poem.

Before we leave these coincidences we may note, perhaps, the recurrence of certain humorous phrases. Several of the characters explain portentously that such-and-such " is the meaning I intended to convey." Two of them confess that they " are not equal to the intellectual pressure of the conversation." Zorah declares that Old Adam loves Dame Hannah " with all the frenzy of a boy of fourteen." Ruth alludes to Frederic when she says that her " love unabated has been accumulating for forty-seven years." " Katisha," declares Ko-Ko, though it is clearly a thumping lie, " for years I have loved you with a white-hot passion that is slowly but surely consuming my very vitals." " When I love," admits Scaphio, and it is with thoughts on an invisible ideal, " it will be with the accumulated fervour of sixty-six years." Grosvenor, more alliterative, declares that he has loved Patience with " a Florentine fourteenth-century frenzy for full fifteen years." In these avowals there is certainly evidence of a ringing of the changes on the same humorous idea.

In the Bab Ballads Gilbert often played with a scheme to link mankind in the bonds of absolute equality. In the operas it is the very widow's cruse of his satirical fancy. It bursts upon us first in " The Sorcerer." Alexis has his plan for encouraging matrimony without any distinctions of rank, and in furtherance of this romantic gospel he has lectured in asylums, workhouses and beershops. Not a man dissented when he urged on a meeting of navvies the advantages of their uniting themselves in marriage with wealthy ladies of rank. And yet it is rather a shock when his prospective mother-in-law, the Lady Sangazure, a dowager of ancient lineage, casts adoring eyes on a cheap sorcerer, John Wellington Wells.

In " H.M.S. Pinafore " the pretty conceit is carried forward a stage. " Love levels rank," insists Captain Corcoran, but his theory has its "inconvenient side " when his daughter, Josephine, falls in love with a common seaman, Ralph Rackstraw. " The line," he then insists, " must be drawn somewhere." The experiment takes a more wholesale form in " The Pirates of Penzance." Major-General Stanley's bevy of daughters are courted by the pirates. Before the curtain falls their suits have succeeded, but it is worth noting that the ladies are not engaged until the pirates are revealed to be members of the House of Lords, nor is Josephine affianced to Ralph Rackstraw until he is found to be, not a common A.B., but the captain of the *Pinafore*. " Love levels rank," which sounded well as a slogan, had seemingly many pitfalls in practice.

" Iolanthe " marks a big advance in the equality comedy. By this time, one must assume, the lower orders have become so inoculated with the new spirit that the nobility is on its defensive, and here is one of its spokesmen actually pleading with a shepherdess not to think too meanly of marriage with one of the gentlemen of England :

> " Spurn not the nobly born
> With love affected,
> Nor treat with virtuous scorn
> The well-connected.
> High rank involves no shame,
> We boast an equal claim
> With him of humble name
> To be respected."

What delicious satire there is in Lord Tolloller's ballad ! It craves a gracious gesture of recognition that hearts just as pure and fair may beat in Belgrave Square as in the lowly air of Seven Dials—not to say in Tooting or Putney.

With " The Gondoliers " matters come to a head. In Barataria all men are equal. " The Noble Lord who rules the State " is as good as and not a whit better than " the Noble Lord who cleans the grate." The gospel of fraternity has never been elevated to such a pinnacle. Yet it is curious that Gilbert, in working up to this climax at last, does not show us how the equality code turns out in practice. All that we can gather about the Baratarians is that brotherhood has made them stingy—do not Marco and Giuseppe complain that, although two personalities, they get rations sufficient only for one ?— and also that they are abrupt and " off-hand " towards these representatives of the Monarchy. Happy-go-lucky though they are, and full of the zest for adventure, the youths are by no means displeased with the prospect of leaving the brotherhood, returning to Venice, and becoming " once more gondolieri, both skilful and wary."

THE EQUALITY COMEDY

It is the Grand Inquisitor who applies the match to the equality theory. The experiment was not original. In days gone by, it seems, it had been tried by a king as benevolent as our more familiar friend, the Mikado. An overwhelming heart had caused him to distribute promotions to all and sundry. And what was the result?

> " Lord Chancellors were cheap as sprats,
> And Bishops in their shovel hats
> Were plentiful as tabby cats—
>   In point of fact, too many ;
> Ambassadors cropped up like hay,
> Prime Ministers and such as they
> Grew like asparagus in May,
>   And Dukes were three a penny."

The moral, as this wise functionary points out, is that when every blessed thing you hold is made of silver or of gold, you long for simple pewter.

" Utopia " has one scene that is reminiscent of " The Gondoliers." The Drawing-room rehearsal, conducted by the Lord Chamberlain, is a variation of the Duke of Plaza-Toro's instruction class with Marco and Giuseppe. In this later opera King Paramount announces that :

" No peeress at our Drawing Room before the Presence
    passes
  Who wouldn't be accepted by the lower-middle classes."

—an obvious re-trimming of a droll line of thought in " Iolanthe." And with this, unless one is mistaken, Gilbert had finished with an over-worked motive for good. The widow's cruse was dry.

CHAPTER XX

SIPS FROM THE CUP

WHAT line of valuation may we apply to the operas ?
I suggest that the most satisfying of them dramatically is " The Yeomen of the Guard," that the most
humorous of them is " The Mikado," that the most
inspiriting of them is " The Gondoliers," that the
most whimsical of them is " Iolanthe," and that the
most satirical of them is " Utopia Limited." So
far as the musical side is concerned, I suggest that
the loveliest melodies are to be found in " Iolanthe,"
the daintiest in " Patience," the most sparkling in
" The Gondoliers," and the happiest in " The
Mikado."

This is purely a tentative summing-up. No one
would be so foolish as to select one work and lay
down dogmatically that it is without question the
greatest. There is no one " best " in Gilbert and
Sullivan. About six of the plays rank fairly
equally. Your liking for one or the other is not so
strong that you make it indisputably the pet of the
family. The " Big Six " I have just mentioned
could be voted on in any large assembly of people,
and one would hazard that, when the personal

preferences had been numbered, no two lists would be identical. Many shrewd judges would object that the vote was invalid because of the exclusion of such an attractive work as " Ruddigore ":

It is true that "The Mikado" is popularly regarded as the masterpiece. If one of the operas must bear this courtesy title it may as well have it. Certainly it is the biggest money-spinner of any of them.[1] It may not be the cleverest piece, but without a doubt it is the merriest one, and with this go its scintillating music and its bright and colourful setting. My own idea is that, if any of us could re-visit the scenes of our earthly pilgrimage two centuries hence, we should see this merry play still hardily defying its years. I have a feeling that in longevity it will wear down every single one of its companions. Its survival value, as an actuary would put it, must be extraordinarily high. " The Gondoliers " has also the elements of permanence.

I say that Gilbert's cleverest work may not be " The Mikado." I suggest that " Iolanthe " has this distinction, not because it is more brilliant in its workmanship, but because of its delightfully fanciful plot. Surely it was an amazing flight of imagination to picture the staid old Mother of Parliaments under the thumbs of the Fairies ! Surely it was an irresistible piece of comedy to suggest that a callow youth from Arcady could take

---

[1] It has been stated, correctly or otherwise, that Gilbert, Sullivan and D'Oyly Carte each drew £30,000 in profits annually from the London and touring productions of *The Mikado*.

control of the legislative machinery, introduce all
the measures he pleased, and upset that British bulwark, the House of Peers, as easily as if it were a
coster's apple-cart!   Surely no other dramatist in
his worst nightmares saw visions of a Lord Chancellor who married an elf and danced by moonlight
in Old Palace Yard, or of a couple of Earls who did
their love-making in public, or of a Grenadier
Guardsman who was transformed into a six-foot
edition of Puck!   What perfectly matchless
audacity!   The Peers' Chorus makes the satire all
the more biting.   The sureness with which the fantastic theme is worked out is extraordinary.

Gilbert is at his best, or nearly at his best, when
his fancy takes a political leaning. " Iolanthe "
and " Utopia " are essentially political operas. And
the most scathing lines he ever wrote are in the
political key.   They are put into Robin Oakapple's
mouth in " Ruddigore " :

" Ye supple M.P.'s, who go down on your knees,
        Your precious identity sinking,
    And vote black or white as your leaders indite
        (Which saves you the trouble of thinking),
    For your country's good fame, her repute, or her shame,
        You don't care the snuff of a candle.
    But you're paid for your game when you're told that your
            name
        Will be graced by a baronet's handle—
    Oh ! allow me to give you a word of advice—
    The title's uncommonly dear at the price ! "

This, of course, is not satire at all, but invective,
cruel and venomous.   The Englishman always did

take a low estimate of his politicians. It is a convention to regard them as self-seeking, sordid-minded, and corrupt. And Gilbert proves himself once more to be a convention-ridden Englishman. I suggest that this is the " hottest " tirade to be found in the operas, and that so far as it adopts a shallow prejudice, and probably an indefensible one, it is itself " uncommonly cheap." The song, which in its place tends to disturb the dramatic sequence, is usually omitted to-day. Perhaps it is as well. There is no reason why politicians should be flayed in this opera.

Here I think we may discuss a few representative scenes in Gilbert and Sullivan. I suggest that the most daring scene is the parody of a Royal Drawing-room in " Utopia." This is the scene in which a Court ceremonial is mimicked in the form of a Christy Minstrel show, and in which King Paramount, having asked whether the " odd " rehearsal is " in accordance with the practice at the Court of St. James's," is informed by one of the Flowers of Progress that it is at least " in accordance with the practice at the Court of St. James's Hall." It is not in good taste, whatever one may think of it, and for once it seems that the licensed satirist had exceeded the bounds that his licence permitted. The most dramatic scene—dramatic solely in its unexpectedness—is the entry of Katisha in " The Mikado." The tenderest scene is Iolanthe's mother-love invocation in " Iolanthe." The most pathetic scene, to me at least, is not Jack Point's final agony,

half artistic and half melodramatic, in " The Yeomen of the Guard."   It is that earlier passage where
the jester, already a broken and disillusioned man,
makes his mournful exit at the end of " When a
wooer goes a-wooing."   There is something in the
situation and in the music that touches genuine
poignancy.   It brings a lump to the throat like
nothing else in the opera.

The most humorous scene cannot be selected so
easily.   A situation which is uncommonly diverting
to one person strikes another indifferently. For my
own part I cannot see anything uproariously funny
in the Penzance Pirates stalking on " with cat-like
tread " and proclaiming the fact fortissimo, nor do
I see anything uncontrollably comic in the sailors
on the *Pinafore* stopping their ears when Ralph
Rackstraw is about to blow out his brains, though I
am told that both these situations are " Gilbertian."
They are a type of situation for which certainly he
had no use in his maturity.   I do see, on the other
hand, the droll side of it when a number of British
lords are in a state of excitement because a shepherd
boy has played ducks and drakes with their Parliamentary prerogatives, and I see the fun of the thing
when those three hulking brutes, the sons of Gama
Rex, solemnly announce that " like all sons are
we, masculine in sex," and when they confess that
" on the whole " they are " not intelligent."   I am
inclined to think that, taking one consideration with
another, as the Sergeant would say, the humorous
scene which appeals to most people is that between

Ko-Ko and Katisha towards the end of " The Mikado." The second best may be the scene, accompanied by delightful music, in which Gama's sons divest themselves of their armour in " Princess Ida." And the third may be the scene in which the three Dragoon officers demonstrate their conversion to aestheticism in " Patience."

Last of all, in this attempt to determine which are the best things of their kind in the operas, what are we to select as the choicest literary passage ? I personally should select Strephon's picturesque defiance of the Lord Chancellor in " Iolanthe " :

" My lord, I know no Courts of Chancery ; I go by Nature's Acts of Parliament. The bees—the breeze—the seas—the rooks—the brooks—the gales—the vales—the fountains and the mountains, cry ' You love this maiden— take her, we command you ! ' 'Tis writ in heaven by the bright barbed dart that leaps forth into lurid light from each grim thunder-cloud. The very rain pours forth her sad and sodden sympathy ! When chorussed Nature bids me take my love, shall I reply, ' Nay, but a certain Chancellor forbids it ' ? Sir, you are England's Lord High Chancellor, but are you Chancellor of birds and trees, King of the winds, and Prince of thunder-clouds ? "

Well may the Lord Chancellor reply that it is a nice point that he has not met with before ! It is an imaginative piece of writing touched by a waft of ironic comedy. And at the same time it is little more than gilded platitude. Most young lovers are guided by Nature's Acts of Parliament, even if it be unconsciously and insensibly.

CHAPTER XXI

TOPICAL ALLUSIONS

Ko-Ko's list of society offenders originally included the lady novelist, whom he described as a singular anomaly, and whom he thought might with the rest " well be underground." Strictly, even in 1885 the lady was not at all singular, nor was she an anomaly. To-day the literary sisterhood might rival the overgrown episcopal family lamented by the Grand Inquisitor. In the later versions of the text the lady is supplanted by the " scorching motorist," a society offender unknown in the early days of " The Mikado," and alternatively by " the sham philanthropist." Private Willis divides mankind from birth into Liberals and Conservatives. The Englishman, however, is less a party man from his cradle on than ever he was, and this piece of military *obiter dicta* goes for nothing in the days of the three-party system. In passing one may note an anachronism connected with the philosophical sentry. Guardsmen are not posted outside the Houses of Parliament.

Gilbert had the wisdom not to be unduly topical. It is the topical allusion that tends to date a play, and when the allusion is a prejudiced one, as that about the lady novelist possibly was, it ages into an absurdity. He did write two plays on topical subjects. " Patience," of course, is one of them, and rarely is it produced without some writer pointing out that aestheticism has long been in its grave. The opera has too much merit for it to be affected by an obsolete theme. " Princess Ida," on the other hand, was never a strong play at its best, and as a skit on women's rights it has grown hoary. Tennyson's poem, on which it is based, may suffer in the same way, but it has high survival value as pure poetry. I do not include " Iolanthe " amongst the topical plays. That opera could be produced hundreds of times without anyone re- membering that it was written during the early Irish Land conflicts and the controversies about the prerogatives of the House of Lords.

" Patience," it is true, is out of date now as regards its main theme, but we need only revise some of its details to make its satire applicable to the foibles and fashions of our own generation. Aestheticism has gone. But Futurism is with us—and it is far less picturesque. Gilded youth no longer favours the velvet suit, but there are modern sartorial affectations, the symbols of the newer foppery. And we have our own Rapturous Maidens. In the spring time, for instance, there are " of damozels a score," armed with their cameras and autograph books, to be seen on the towing-paths at Putney. They are to be seen in many other places where they can offer their distant worship to the glorious Apollo. The rapture now is for athleticism rather than for art, for physical vigour rather than for poetical fervour, and it is an altogether healthier thing.

We may add to the obsolete phrases mentioned in the opening paragraph. " Iolanthe," for instance, has a reference to " that annual blister, marriage with deceased wife's sister," a debatable matter which, to use the Queen's word, has now been finally " pricked." In the same opera there is the reference to Captain Shaw, a name only to this generation, though he was the organiser and first chief of the Metropolitan Fire Brigade. Captain Shaw it was who raised fire-fighting from a primitive makeshift, mainly financed by the insurance offices, into a great public service, and it is odd that he should have immortality chiefly through a beautiful song. " The Mikado " has a reference to the six-hour sermons of " mystical Germans." They are no longer with us. Nor, less fortunately, are Madame Tussaud's or those delightful chamber concerts, the " Monday Pops." An allusion to the old penny readings, also not of our day, occurs in both the " Sorcerer " and " Ruddigore."

The " Heavy Dragoon " song in " Patience " is littered with names hardly familiar to this generation, though that fact, to be sure, does little harm to such a rollicking song. For instance, there is a reference to a famous private detective of his time

named Pollaky, a man of " keen penetration " who
had his offices at Paddington Green, and who was
known to the public as " Paddington Pollaky."
There is a reference to Jullien, a popular light
orchestra conductor in Gilbert's youth, and another
to Dion Boucicault, whose Irish plays and his own
acting in them give point to the line about " the
pathos of Paddy." There is the reference to
D'Orsay,[1] the dandy and wit whose personality
Gilbert apparently associated with " quackery,"
partly because he was a notoriously vain man, but
mainly because the word provided a convenient
rhyme for " Dickens and Thackeray." King Victor
Emmanuel, of course, was one of the creators, with
Cavour and Garibaldi, of modern Italy. The
allusion to Dr. Sacheverell recalls to us the
eighteenth-century divine whose printed sermons
were publicly burnt at the Royal Exchange. The
Lord Waterford who is described as reckless and
rollicky belonged to the old school of sportsmen.
And " The Stranger, a touch of him " refers to the
title-part in a play which attracted many leading
tragedians down to the time of Wilson Barrett.

In all there are nearly a couple of score of names
mentioned in this remarkable song.[2] They include
statesmen like Bismarck and that famous French

[1] Count A. G. G. D'Orsay, the sculptor and painter, was born in
Paris, but early in Queen Victoria's reign he was the supreme arbiter of
London's fashions. He was an extremely handsome man.

[2] Dr. T. Stephenson, to whom fitting acknowledgment is made for
many of the facts here given, provided the full glossary of the song in
the *Gilbert and Sullivan Journal*, July 1926.

197

Parliamentary orator of the Second Empire, Guizot ; great captains like Cæsar and Hannibal, Nelson and Wolseley ; and distinguished men of letters like Fielding, Macaulay, Dickens, Thackeray, Tennyson, Defoe, and Trollope. In a greater or lesser degree they may all be classed as " remarkable people in history." It is more difficult, however, to find this justification for the inclusion of the uniformed beadle of the Burlington Arcade or that of Richardson's show, the garish frontage of which was once familiar at the old fairs, though changes and improvements in the popular taste had proved too much for these entertainments even before the time of the writing of " Patience." Still less does one see the point of resemblance between them and the dashing military superman known to the world as the Heavy Dragoon.

" Ruddigore " shows its age in one peculiar way. The " Darned Mounseer " is a fine song, and it is not inappropriate to the opera, the period of which is the early nineteenth century. No little anti-French sentiment survived even in 1887, when the work was produced, and the words of the ballad revealed the traditional contempt for the foreigner, though many people missed the finer shades of Gilbert's satirical thrust at the expense of the insular Englishman. Nevertheless, at the risk of being thought captious, one may question whether such a song would ever be tolerated in a new opera, even an historical light opera, to-day. I say this fully conscious that its omission would rob us of one of the brightest features, and incomparably one of the best airs, with its dramatic hornpipe sequel, that this opera possesses :

" She's only a darned Mounseer,
            D'ye see ?
She's only a darned Mounseer !
But to fight a French fal-lal—it's like hittin' of a gal—
    It's a lubberly thing for to do ;
        For we, with all our faults,
        Why, we're sturdy British salts,
    While she's only a Parley-voo,
            D'ye see ?
    While she's only a Parley-voo ! "

I have had something to say already about the women characters in the operas. I return to this matter merely to suggest that here is another symptom of antiquity. Gilbert's women are not the women of this generation. They are hardly, indeed, true portraits of those of his own day, but their pallid shallowness, their lack of personality, bears no resemblance whatever to the modern maid, that lively creature who is self-reliant from her bobbed head to her toes. Some of the Gilbert young ladies complain of the " vapours." That also, trivial as it is, date-stamps the operas. There is the scene in which those bashful twins, Nekaya and Kalyba, figure in the first act of " Utopia." Standing, the picture of *naïveté*, with their hands folded and their eyes cast down, they are supposed to represent the model English girl of the period, " demurely modest, divinely cold." If this were to be taken as satire, and thus to have the half-truth that all good satire possesses, it would show once more how widely conditions have changed since these operas began. Actually this scene is just clever extravagance. Gilbert tells us what he thinks of the English girl later on when her praises are extolled by one of the Flowers of Progress. The amend is handsome indeed.

Let me here put in just a word of explanation. If I have enumerated a few obsolescences which are to be found in the text on present-day reading, it has been to show that the list, so far from being a large one, is uncommonly small. They are not cracks, they are not even fissures, in the dramatic structure of the plays. They are so few that we are almost unconscious of them. Gilbert and Sullivan would have worn less well had the dramatist indulged a pleasant passion for the topical.

It is profitable to turn to the other side of the account. Some names and allusions there may be which, as a medium of humour, have lost a little of their piquancy. A number of words and phrases, on the other hand, have been added to the vocabulary. In their different ways they belong to the currency of common speech. " Gilbertian " is one of them. As applied to any droll situation, any piece of quaintly-inverted logic, any comic upheaval of the conventions, the word is immediately self-expressive. A " Gilbertian idea " must always be laughable. An idea which is merely twisted or illogical, and which does not invite a smile, does not properly fall within this category. The Gilbertian flavour is not in it. " Pooh-Bah " as a name has also found its way into the language. It typifies the pluralist, the holder of many offices, though we do not require that, like his prototype, he should necessarily hold them for profit.

Here are a few every-day phrases, arranged approximately to popularity, which come from the operas :

" The policeman's lot is not a happy one."
" The flowers that bloom in the spring, tra-la-la ! "
" To make the punishment fit the crime."
" No probable, possible shadow of doubt, no possible doubt whatever."
" I've got a little list."
" When everyone is somebodee, then no one's anybody."

I do not suggest, of course, that these exhaust the common quotations, though they may be the outstanding examples. A diligent student, confining his researches to about half-a-dozen papers, has discovered that on the average they had one quotation from the operas for every week of the year. Some of the references, it must be admitted, were not easily recognisable, and the writers had shown a wider familiarity with the plays than that possessed by the ordinary man, whose unconscious tribute to them we are at the moment considering. So far as my own list is concerned, it will be noticed that most of these over-worked phrases are platitudes, and also that the people who use them usually do so with a humorous application. Don Alhambra's lines about there being no possible doubt are the mere elaboration of the obvious—a verbose indication that some statement is conclusive and final. And yet the recital of all these words has often an effect that is curiously funny.

I suppose I shall not be challenged in selecting as the most quoted Gilbert phrase the Sergeant's mournful reflection in " The Pirates of Penzance." One meets with it continually. Sometimes it occurs in its direct form in relation to the police. It may or may not be true that the policeman's lot is not a happy one, but undoubtedly it is a happier lot now with the higher prestige that the constabulary service enjoys, the more generous rates of pay, and the comfortable scale of pensions. That is a detail we need not trouble to argue. The phrase is also used a great deal indirectly. " Like the policeman's, the lot of the blank is not a happy one," recurs with variations in conversation and print, though here, like Ko-Ko, " the task of filling in the blank I'd rather leave to you."

Gilbert and Sullivan both had an affection for the real-life policeman. Gilbert often introduced him in the Bab Ballads. He is made a comic figure as a rule, and in the one opera in which he appears, the picture of him, to be frank, is not complimentary. It is one of several instances in which the humorous and musical treatment of an idea have to be taken together. Some rather biting bit of humour, as it may be standing alone, becomes an inoffensive and jocular affair when the music is wedded to it, and so gives completeness to a droll and happy conception. Craven as they may be—if we are absurd enough to take the satire of it too seriously—there is something rather flattering in the picture of the policemen in " The Pirates of Penzance." They exude warm-hearted benevolence. They see the divine streak in the most uncouth of the criminal kind :

> " When the enterprising burglar's not a-burgling,
> When the cut-throat isn't occupied in crime,
> He loves to hear the little brook a-gurgling,
> And listen to the merry village chime.
> When the coster's finished jumping on his mother,
> He loves to lie a-basking in the sun.
> Ah !   Take one consideration with another,
> The policeman's lot is not a happy one."

Somehow the logic of these last lines seems to go a little astray.   It is not clear why this idyll of the sentimental criminal in his hours of ease should fill the honest constabulary heart with dejection.

Sullivan never concealed his admiration for the London policeman, and this probably dated back to the time when he was a young organist at St. Michael's, Chester Square.   Near the church was a police station, and when there were no constabulary duties to be done, the officers often attended the Sunday services, and also a special service held for them every Wednesday.   The adult choir was composed mainly of policemen. Sullivan, it is said, found them raw material at the beginning, but he had a wonderful way with him,

203

and he turned them into a choir almost second to none. He had, of course, the handling of many bodies of choristers, but one would like to think that it was the experience he gained with this policemen's choir that helped him most of all in his greater days at the Savoy.

CHAPTER XXII

GILBERT'S LOVE SCENES

I HAVE said elsewhere that Gilbert's long suit was not his humanity. There is evidence of this in his love scenes. Every opera has a little love-making in public, but it is the kind that suggests that the dramatist, who tilted at many conventions, had not the courage to defy the romantic conventions that are part of a play. The public likes the sentimental touch on the stage. It asks for the tender passion, in one form or another, to be put on parade, and the more ecstatic it is, the more satisfying the thrill that drifts over the footlights. Gilbert could not afford to leave the love element out, and to do him justice, he was not so hard-crusted as to bid the lover begone. But the fact remains that his love scenes are unconvincing. He never wrote a "Romeo and Juliet," or anything like it, and he never wrote an opera in which the love motive was other than subsidiary.

Now, when one thinks of it, this is rather surprising. Gilbert, like most men, had a strain of sentiment in him, though to the outer world it was

disguised. The lyrics that in diverse forms exalt
the truth that

> " It were profanity
> For poor humanity
> To treat as vanity
>   The sway of love "

are often exquisite things. They enshrine the
idealism of it in beautiful imagery and the choicest
language. But when it comes to the love situations
there is an extraordinary change. The poet is
shown the door and the jester begins his old capers
again. Sometimes the effect is unfortunate—or
unfortunate if, even in a stage play, one appreciates
sincerity. A playwright must be allowed incon-
sistencies that would not, for instance, be allowed
to a novelist, who has more scope for working out
his ideas in an orderly way. Gilbert, nevertheless,
has a habit at times of soaring into the rapturous
heights, and then volting down, breathless fashion,
into absurdity. I have in mind one particular case
in the operas. We have a serene and tender duet,
as lovely as the mind of a poet ever conceived, and
then a few minutes later we find that the sentiment
of it is contradicted and the sweet idealism destroyed.

The opera is " Iolanthe." The lovers are
Strephon and Phyllis. They sing, I repeat, a most
beautiful and haunting duet, full of picturesque
simile and of vows of eternal fealty. In another
chapter I give this number high place amongst the
best songs in the operas. Singing to a melody

which unerringly matches the sentiment, and which shows that the words are seriously meant, the lovers profess how :

> " None shall part us from each other,
>   One in life and death are we :
> All in all to one another,
>   I to thee and thou to me ! "

Yet within a few minutes Phyllis, piqued at seeing Strephon with a lady who is really his uncommonly young-looking mother, has announced that she will fling her heart at either of the Noble Lords who will have her, and when *she* returns to her senses, then Strephon abruptly turns *his* back on his Phyllis. It may be only a lovers' tiff—we know all comes right in the end—and it may be that it is " only an opera." But it does show that the eternal love vow of the lyric rang falsely. The attachment, which we thought so idyllic, is really so slender that the girl breaks matters off, and on their wedding day too, without awaiting from her lover one word of explanation. I know that we should treat these romantic vagaries indulgently. The point is that this situation lets down badly the ethereal tone of the lyric. The poet has enchanted us—and along comes the jester and drags us back to mundanity. This is not a good example of Gilbert's virtue of " unexpectedness."

If a lyric of itself could make a love scene, or if the incidents which lead up to this lyric were in keeping with it, then one would have ventured to say that here was the best love scene in the operas.

But a lyric alone cannot make a scene, and the dialogue which precedes this is not romantic, its theme being concerned mainly with politics. And so where must one turn to find the most tender and exquisite idyll ? " Patience " in this matter is profitless. The Patience-Grosvenor affair is no more than a verbal skirmish. For the moment I dismiss the case of Bunthorne and Lady Jane. Gilbert has a number of these sere and yellow matches scattered about the operas, and each of them, as we shall see presently, serves the purpose merely of absurdity. The usual picture is that of a dogged spinster and some old fool who is content to set her ancient heart throbbing.

" The Yeomen of the Guard " has not a real love scene. I mean by this a scene where the grand passion is genuinely stirring. It is strange that this is so, because there is more romance here, accepting the term widely, than in any other opera. Certainly there is no endearing scene between Jack Point and Elsie Maynard. Colonel Fairfax has a short love scene of sorts with the girl. Known to himself, but unknown to her, it is a case of a husband wooing his wife, and a husband, as he explains, does not get such a chance every day. It was only a few minutes earlier that this philanderer had bemoaned the " cursed haste " that had placed him in " conjugal fetters." During those strange nuptials in the Tower his bride had been blindfolded, and when he sees her pretty face, he seems to think he has not made such a bad bargain. Fairfax is the type of man who would judge only by surface appearance. So that he might spite his relative, he had married beneath him, clearly not of his own choice, and ostracism would surely have been the penalty in those days of the scion of a great family who married a common strolling player. The conspiracy that had saved him from the block had probably doomed him to life-long social tragedy.

Let us continue the search for the best love scene. We get no satisfaction in " The Sorcerer." We look in vain for it in " The Pirates of Penzance." " Patience " is empty, " Iolanthe " is disappointing, and there is too much feminine chilly-heartiness in " Princess Ida." In " The Mikado " there are few sweet intimacies between Nanki-Poo and Yum-Yum. Here Gilbert makes play with a whimsical idea which re-appears with more effect in " The Gondoliers." " Modified rapture ! " exclaims Nanki-Poo when he hears that his sweetheart, though about to be married to another man, does not love him. And then, because the Mikado's edict has made flirting a crime, the two of them exchange sentimental sighs from opposite sides of the stage. This, of course, is a good Gilbertian situation, but it is the only romantic incident between Nanki-Poo and Yum-Yum. Perhaps it goes far enough. No nicely-brought-up young lady ought to exchange amorous glances with a young gentleman who is not her groom on her very wedding day. And at this point Yum-Yum is to be married to Ko-Ko.

The best love scene, I am inclined to think, is that between Luiz and Casilda in " The Gondoliers." The revelation that they are lovers is delightfully unexpected. Gilbert introduces one of his favourite complications. Casilda's romantic dream has to be shattered by the revelation that she is married already. It was a parental match contrived for her in her infancy. For the meekness of some of these Gilbert young ladies one cannot withhold a sneaking regard. Yum-Yum is to be married to her guardian, whom she does not like at all, and yet she has not the pluck to complain. Casilda, too, has a young man of her own, but when her parents introduce another party entirely, one might have expected her, at the very least, to stamp her little foot or say that it was highly provoking. A modern miss would have done it and said it—and more. Casilda must be accepted as the very model of a dutiful daughter.

The love scene with Luiz, attractive though it is, falls into line with Nanki-Poo's idea of " modified rapture." There is humour in it, there is a pretty sentiment in it, and there is also a touch of gentle pathos. Notice the blend of the whimsical and the wistful in this choice little passage :

Luiz : My own—that is, until ten minutes since, my own—my lately loved, my recently adored—tell me that until, say a quarter of an hour ago, I was all in all to thee (*embracing her*).

Casilda : I see your idea. It's ingenious, but don't do that (*releasing herself*).

Luiz : There can be no harm in revelling in the past.

Casilda : None whatever, but an embrace cannot be taken to act retrospectively.

Luiz : Perhaps not !

Casilda : We may recollect an embrace—I recollect many—but we must not repeat them.

Luiz : Then let us recollect a few ! (*A moment's pause, as they recollect, then both heave a deep sigh*).

And so on.   It is a quaint idea, this idea that these two lovers can be lovers no longer, but that they do not offend the proprieties by sitting in company and revelling in their remembrances only.   I suggest that this is the best, just as it is probably the oddest, love scene in the operas.   It closes on the mournful note of that beautiful lyric :

> " Oh, bury, bury—let the grave close o'er.
>   The days that were—that never will be more ;
>   Oh, bury, bury love that all condemn,
>   And let the whirlwind mourn its requiem."

A lovely fragment—despite the strained rhyme. And, really, the sighing was all for nothing. Casilda has to surrender Luiz, the ducal drummer, because she has been married by proxy in babyhood to— this same Luiz, the lost Baratarian Heir-Apparent. In " The Gondoliers " also we have two instances literally of love at first sight.   Marco and Giuseppe choose their brides by the aid of a merry game of blind-man's-buff.   No sooner have the handker- chiefs been removed from their eyes than they pro- claim that in Tessa and Gianetta they have found " just the very girls they wanted."   There is no love scene. They rush off and get married without further parley. For the rest of the opera they appear before us as young married couples. They give the impression that, though married in hot haste, they will have no cause for leisured repentance.

I like the love scene between Fitzbattleaxe and Zara in " Utopia." It is a comic scene, but there is a good deal of romance implied in it, especially when the adoring lady listens to the confession, with dreadful vocal illustrations, that a tenor in love cannot do himself justice :

> " A tenor, all singers above
>   (This doesn't admit of a question)
>   Should keep himself quiet,
>   Attend to his diet
>   And carefully nurse his digestion ;
> But when he's madly in love
>   It's certain to tell on his singing ;
>   You can't do chromatics
>   With proper emphatics
>   When anguish your bosom is wringing ! "

—a sympathetic concession to a race of men for whom, it must be confessed, the dramatist's opinion was never profound.[1]

Looking at many of Gilbert's early plays, one notices how well he could speak the language of

---

[1] In an interview that appeared in the *Daily Telegraph* in 1909, Gilbert said of tenors " They never can act and they are more trouble than all the members of the company put together. The tenor has been the curse of every piece I have written."

love, and one can only speculate why the romantic embers burn so low in the operas. Was it because in these later years the inspiration was lacking ? Was it because sentiment was held in check by the narrower limits of a musical play ? Was it because he could touch a loftier note in verse than he ever could in dialogue ? Or was it because in the operas he had at all costs to be funny ? Perhaps for the answer to the riddle we must take these reasons together. Certainly I could have quoted many more cases where the sweetest and tenderest of sentiments are enshrined in his lyrics. But it is dialogue, after all, which usually carries on the action of the play, and if a couple of lovers cannot help on the action, then they must be hurried off the stage. He had no time to spare for spectacular love-making just for the " look of the thing." There is too much action to be got through. I would illustrate this by the case of Alexis and Aline in "The Sorcerer." When we first meet them this newly-engaged couple are not allowed to be " sloppy." The conversation between them has to carry forward the plot. It is certainly a business-like method of writing a play.

The " September " marriages in the operas are numerous, but there is precious little romance about them, and usually they hold up to mockery the type of faded spinster who clings desperately to a fast-departing youth.[1] The best love scene of this class is that between Sir Roderic and Dame Hannah in

[1] See Dark and Grey's *W. S. Gilbert : His Life and Letters.*

"Ruddigore." It has real charm, but the charm comes, not from the situation, which is weak, but from the lovely parable-duet of the flower and the oak tree. The drollest love scene so-called is that between Ko-Ko and Katisha in "The Mikado." If, indeed, one could judge this solely from the standpoint of a well-drawn scene with any amount of first-class humour, one might describe it as the very best in the operas. The saddest love scene, so far as it merits any romantic description, is that wherein Shadbolt claims Phœbe in "The Yeomen of the Guard." This repulsive creature gains the staunch little woman as the price of her honourable folly. As a match-maker Gilbert never did worse than to link such an impossible pair.

Frankly, it is a dismal business to draw up a list of those pertinacious old maids who scramble into wedlock, because the humour is usually cheap. Little Buttercup makes a match with ex-Captain Corcoran in "H.M.S Pinafore." Lady Jane makes a reckless bid for Bunthorne before the Duke takes her in "Patience" solely as a reward for her "plainness." Dame Carruthers gets Sergeant Meryll as the price of her silence in "The Yeomen of the Guard." King Paramount is caught in Lady Sophy's net in "Utopia." There may be other cases. There is that strange union of high-born fairy and low-born mortal in the case of the Queen and Private Willis at the end of "Iolanthe." You will remember that the Queen pops the question. "Well, ma'am," answers that worthy fellow, "I don't think much of a British soldier who wouldn't ill-convenience himself to save a female in distress."

There are several Gilbert characters who share with the British soldier this quixotic sense of gallantry.

CHAPTER XXIII

BUNTHORNE AND GROSVENOR

In " Patience " you may find the receipt for that popular mystery known to the world as a Heavy Dragoon. Gilbert and Sullivan is also a popular mystery. It is surely nothing less than a mystery that there should be such popular vitality and hardiness in plays which in themselves are so slender and simple. Like the Dragoon of the song, it is a compound of many excellencies, and if only a new school of comic opera could arise and " take of these elements all that is fusible," we might yet see in our own time a revival of the old glories of the Savoy.

The " receipt " for it you may find, or try to find, in the same opera. " Patience " may not be the cleverest play, but there is none in which the dramatist and the composer, separately or combined, appear to greater advantage. It is Gilbert and Sullivan in its most representative form, the model which would-be imitators should study all day in methodical way, not because it is necessarily the best play, but because it contains so much that is typical of the genius of the two partners.

" Patience " carries us into an artificial atmosphere and its subject is hackneyed.   But the fact
remains that nowhere else is the wit so brilliant or
the music so enchanting.   Gilbert's satire is never
more vigorous, his rhyming more ingenious, his
lyrics more charming.   The libretto is written with
a sure hand and with no little gusto.   And Sullivan
here is wonderful also.   There can be no doubt
about that.   The " Patience " music is the sweetest,
the most bountifully inspired, of all the music he
wrote, and some of it pays high tribute to his technical gifts in orchestral and choral craftsmanship.

We have seen that a feature of Gilbert's humour
is its bent towards rotund phraseology.   At times
also it makes a swoop from mock gravity into
absurdity.   A good instance occurs in Lady Jane's
line about a " transcendentality of delirium, an
acute accentuation of supremest ecstasy, which the
earthly might easily mistake for indigestion."   Of
necessity the words put into the mouths of the
aesthetics are extravagant.   The construction of
that sentence, nevertheless, is after the dramatist's
heart.   So, too, is the incident wherein one of the
aesthetics speaks about " the Inner Brotherhood,
perceptively intense and consummately utter,"
whatever. that farrago may mean, and is countered
by the materialistic inquiry, " What does the Inner
Brotherhood usually recommend for cramp ? "

In " Patience " also Gilbert's talent for nimble
versification is seen at its very happiest.   Bunthorne's first song is a particularly clever piece of

writing. Note also how easily there trip from the tongue such lines as

" Overcome your diffidence and natural timidity,
   Tickets for the raffle should be purchased with avidity "

and

" I was the beau ideal of the morbid young aesthetical,
   To doubt my inspiration was regarded as heretical.
   Until you cut me out with your placidity emetical "

—two first-class examples of his gift for multi-syllabic jugglery.

" Patience " should be a melancholy opera. The poets, the love-lorn ladies, and to some extent the soldiers, bemoan their state of misery. And yet misery never paraded itself more joyously. The opera, which has not one hearty character in it, is hearty and stimulating all the way through. It runs perilously near to the border-line of farce, but never does it become farce, and never does the handling seem to become inartistic or limp. In every phase of this brilliant play there is elegance. The opening scene is an exquisite picture. The grouping of the rapturous maidens has a classic grace. The serenity of their music heightens the contrast that occurs with the arrival of those " fleshly men of full habit "—the 35th Dragoon Guards.

Except that they both dress in velvets, and except also that they are both miserable beings, there is little similarity between Bunthorne and Grosvenor. The poets make a delightfully contrasted couple. Bunthorne is a mountebank, an intellectual charlatan, a self-advertising humbug. Grosvenor is the Apostle of Simplicity. Bunthorne professes very truly that he is " highly spiced." Grosvenor is tame and insipid. Bunthorne is the superlative egotist. He cannot live without admiration. Grosvenor, on the other hand, finds the surfeit of admiration cloying. Nature has endowed this bashful man with physical perfection, and he endures the admiration of his fellow-creatures, not at all because he likes it, but because it is his duty in life to be a faithful trustee for beauty.

Bunthorne is no Adonis. He is bilious, but not, we are assured, as bilious as he looks. Like most of Gilbert's characters, he is amazingly frank when he is alone with his audience, and we have his own confession that he is a hypocrite. It is only to gratify a morbid love of admiration that he has devised his plan to " lie upon the daisies and discourse in novel phrases." He is, in common language, a spoofer. Grosvenor is a man with a mission. Bunthorne's mission is merely that of self-glorification, and an overwhelming vanity has made him discontented, neurotic and petulant.

" Do you know what it is to be heart hungry ? Do you know what it is to yearn for the indefinable and yet to be brought face to face with the multiplication table ? Do you know what it is to seek oceans and to find puddles—to long for whirlwinds and to have to do the best you can with the bellows ? That's my case. Oh ! I am a cursed thing ! "

Grosvenor, although he does not say so himself, is also a cursed thing. There is no need for him to

carry a poppy or a lily as he walks down Piccadilly.
He is beautiful without floral aid or adornment.
He gazes in the mirror and finds that he is indeed
a very narcissus. The consciousness of it gives
no cause for boasting. Grosvenor, a paragon of
masculine loveliness, is also a paragon of modesty.
It is his " hideous destiny " to be loved madly by
every woman he meets, but he cannot escape it by
disguising himself, nor by making himself less
picturesque. That would make him false to his
trust as a witness to beauty. Fair admirers have
followed him about from Tuesday to Saturday. He
craves the boon of his usual half-holiday. The
burden has made him, not an embittered man, but
rather a sad and a reproachful one, inasmuch as his
fatal perfection is for ever interposing between him
and happiness.

Bunthorne is without a doubt the more gifted
poet. Not for Grosvenor is the classic diction of
calomel and colocynth. *He* cannot rise above
doggerel about a very bad boy whose end it was
to be " lost *totally* " and to be married to " a girl in
the *corps de bally*." But this " smug-faced idiot "—
and there is little wrong with his rival's description
except the adjective—is possibly the more original
type. We have Bunthornes in real life, charlatans
who attach themselves to all kinds of movements,
and who use their wits to thrust themselves into
prominence. Grosvenor is a weird, effeminate
creature whom we have never met in this world,
and if he were not a man of property, we should

wonder how such a dotard could ever earn his living. The one sensible thing about him is his transformation at the end of the opera. He cuts his hair, wears the loudest of checks, and becomes as sprightly as he has been languid. The change is violent to a degree. Grosvenor, the idyllic poet, has become " clerky." He has descended to bottled beer and chops. And Gilbert uses the chop more than once as the symbol of the absolutely commonplace.

Patience herself is also a novel type. She has, on the evidence of the text, reached the age of eighteen or twenty. But she has never heard of love, she sees it only as a malady that is strangely upsetting, and she inquires how it is to be distinguished from insanity. In her sense of duty she is the petticoat counterpart of a certain pirate apprentice. She is led to accept love as a duty. But this love must be an unselfish emotion. And here we find Gilbert exploiting a favourite line of his—a line which we may describe as the argumentative quibble. Patience is ready to love Grosvenor—and love him with a " heart-whole ecstasy that withers, and scorches, and burns, and stings." Suddenly she recoils in horror.

Grosvenor : What's the matter ?
Patience : Why, you are perfection, a source of endless ecstasy to all who know you !
Grosvenor: I know I am. Well ?
Patience : Then, bless my heart, there can be nothing unselfish in loving *you* !
Grosvenor : Merciful Powers ! I never thought of that.

Patience : To monopolise those features on which all women love to linger ! It would be unpardonable.

Grosvenor : Why, so it would ! Oh ! fatal perfection again you interpose between me and my happiness.

Patience : Oh ! if you were but a thought less beautiful than you are !

Grosvenor : Would that I were, but candour compels me to admit that I'm not.

Patience : Our duty is clear : we must part, and for ever.

Grosvenor : Oh ! misery ! And yet I cannot question the propriety of your decision. Farewell !

And so, for the time being, they part. At no cost would a Gilbert and Sullivan young lady do the unpardonable thing ! Later, when Grosvenor has transformed himself into a commonplace young man, and when it would no longer be selfish to claim him to the exclusion of all other women, the maidenly scruples have gone. These situations bear the authentic Gilbert hall-mark.

Before we leave the characters we must pay a passing reference to the troopers. During the first act we hear these stalwarts proclaiming that they are a combination of the virtues of all the people famous in history. There never were such soldier-like paragons—or such profoundly boastful ones—as these Heavy Dragoons. They shower a withering contempt on the " peripatetics of long-haired aesthetics." Yet in the second act the officers, whom we have been led to believe had no equals on earth, have become aesthetic disciples. The paragons are discovered practising the stained-glass window attitudes. " By stations of three," rings

out the command, " rapture ! " And smartly these
military men strike a rapturous pose—a diverting
bit of by-play. The reason for their conversion
is that they are engaged to the ladies who have
been " idealised " by Bunthorne, and they become
angular and flat, not at all from enthusiasm or conviction, but solely as a means of making a " lasting
impression."

Musically the opera is flawless, a lovely sequence
of beautiful tunes, and all of them fitting so perfectly
that words and music seem to be, as it were, one
inspiration. " The Silver Churn " is in my judgment the best melody, and the song itself one of the
best songs, in Gilbert and Sullivan Opera. " Prithee,
Pretty Maiden," a still simpler and more delicate
one, would satisfy even those artistic souls who crave
for the " Early English." " I hear the soft note "
illustrates the composer's gift in applying ecclesiastic
harmonies to the service of the stage. " Silvered is
the raven hair " shows how he could give charm to
a lyric which, judged by itself, might seem neither
generous nor gracious. A perfect little gem of
melody redeems the incident—and as an incident
it *is* rather absurd !—of the mock tears of the
troopers. And then there is the big double chorus
in the first act, the soldiers singing in sharp, resentful
tones their denunciation of the " pretty sort of treatment for a military man " while the maidens are
singing the tranquil supplications of " Mystic poet,
hear our prayer." The writing of this ensemble,
with its contrast of moods and its broad climax, is

masterly. In the finale to the first act there is a lively imitation of Verdi.

I have tried to show that " Patience " contains some of the best of Gilbert and some, and more than some, of the best of Sullivan. I hold that, while it is not necessarily the best opera, it is certainly the most representative one, that it contains all the elements that are characteristic of each and both of them, and that it shows how complementary they were as dramatist and composer. Now and then in these works it seems that Gilbert " lets down " Sullivan. It is rare that he does so—and it is rarer still for Sullivan to let down Gilbert. In " Patience " at all events the unity is perfect.

CHAPTER XXIV

THE SIX BEST LYRICS

It is not an easy matter to select the six best songs in the operas. In any case the choice is bound to be guided by personal preference. A greater difficulty still is that of the standard we are to apply. Shall we judge a song by its virtue as poetry, by its metrical ingenuity, by its comedy or sentiment, by its singable qualities, or by its association with some favourite part? I think the test of merit must be all of these factors. My aim at the moment is to dissociate the words from the music, though it is clear that this is a counsel of perfection, an ideal to which it is impossible to be faithful in practice. The very mention of a Gilbert song inevitably calls to mind the melody with which it is coupled. The lyric and the music must go together. Separated, each loses a little, but the loss to the lyric is of necessity greater.

In approaching this subject I have thought it well to divide the songs into groups. The classification is a rough one, possibly an arbitrary one, but it offers the framework for a preparatory survey. I have made groups, for instance, of what we may call for convenience the biographical songs, the narrative songs, the pathetic songs and the philosophical songs. It is unnecessary to have any group of purely comic songs. There are also the songs which appeal by their picturesqueness of simile or beauty of thought. It is these picturesque songs that come nearest of all to real poetry. The genuine poetry of some of them cannot be questioned.

The biographical songs—and we are taking songs to include concerted numbers and choruses—make a large group. In this class are the songs with which the chief characters sketch their careers in life or offer candid comments on their personalities. We find the first of these in " Trial by Jury." The Judge's song is without a doubt a great song, full of lively humour and an amazing frankness, and it gives a complete pen-picture of this unblushing judicial jobber. If we could note how the music enriches the irony—and that is just what we have said we must not do—we should agree that it is an exceptionally great song. I will disclose at once that in my final list this number will have a high place.

In " The Sorcerer " we reach Dr. Daly's " Time was when love and I were well acquainted." It has the form of a wistful reverie, and it has a charm, a modest quietness, not so evident in the other biographical songs. In " H.M.S. Pinafore " we have Sir Joseph Porter's " Stick close to your desks," another candid song which has an obvious resemblance to, though it is less cynical than, the

Judge's outburst in " Trial by Jury." The Lord Chancellor's " When I went to the Bar " is one of the best numbers in " Iolanthe." In " Princess Ida " Gama has a self-revealing character sketch rather than an autobiography. In " The Mikado " we have two gruesomely-humorous songs that are biographical only by anticipation. They are those in which Ko-Ko and the Mikado outline their aims —merely a pious aim in one case, a more concrete one in the other—of exterminating certain amiable sinners from the body politic. If the Mikado's song, a very fine one, is omitted from the final list, it will be omitted by only the narrowest margin.

A few of the biographical ditties I propose to include amongst the patter songs. Here we discover Gilbert as a versifier of uncommon adroitness. We have " My name is John Wellington Wells " in " The Sorcerer," " I am a very model of a modern Major-General " in " The Pirates of Penzance," Bunthorne's " If you're anxious for to shine " and the two Dragoon songs in " Patience," the Lord Chancellor's nightmare song in " Iolanthe," the Duke of Plaza-Toro's " In enterprise of martial kind " in " The Gondoliers," and Rudolph's " A pattern to professors of monarchical autonomy " in " The Grand Duke." I must discard all but Colonel Calverley's " Heavy Dragoon." In this the topical references and the awkward rhymes are handled with extraordinary facility. The massive conceit to which this song gives expression must not be ignored.

I do not think there will be much doubt about the best love song. It is the " Iolanthe " duet between Strephon and Phyllis. In beautiful imagery it is a matchless piece of poetic writing :

> " All in all since that fond meeting,
>> When, in joy, I woke to find
> Mine the heart within thee beating,
>> Mine the love that heart enshrined !
> Thou the stream and I the willow
>> Thou the sculptor, I the clay,
> Thou the ocean, I the billow,
>> Thou the sunrise, I the day ! "

In a plaintive vein there are many beautiful songs. Phœbe's " Were I thy bride " is possibly the best of them if we judge by the lyric. To my mind there is none that sounds such depths of human feeling. Phœbe's earlier " When maiden sits " is another of those instances in which a good lyric is heightened in effect by a surpassingly attractive melody. " Iolanthe's " " He loves ! If in the bygone years," appealing though it may be, also owes much to the tenderness of the musical accompaniment. I fear, too, that the same must be said about that great " Yeomen of the Guard " quartet, " When a wooer goes a-wooing." Gianetta's " Kind sir, you cannot have the heart," Josephine's " Sorry her lot who loves too well," and Katisha's " Hearts do not break " are one and all noteworthy as regards poetical value and sincerity. " I have a song to sing O," another of the plaintive songs, is in the nature of an allegory. It is a very beautiful and ingenious lyric.   In any list of the twenty best songs its exclusion would be impossible.

What I call the philosophical songs are those which explore a line of popular philosophy. Colonel Fairfax has one of the best of them in " Is life a boon ? "   A lyric of this class must lend distinction to the popular stage.   Nearest to it in the same category come " Try we life-long " in " The Gondoliers "—this is the number that invites us to string the lyre and fill the cup, lest on sorrow we should sup—and Gilbert's song of high endeavour, the " Utopia " unaccompanied chorus " Eagle high in cloudland soaring."

> " Let the eagle, not the sparrow,
>   Be the object of your arrow,
>   Fix the tiger with your eye,
>   Pass the fawn in pity by ;
>   Glory then will crown the day,
>   Glory, glory, anyway."

The narrative songs are those which have a direct part in the unfolding of the dramatic plot. Here again I am singling out only a few numbers that may be taken into account in the final selection. Giuseppe's " Rising early in the morning " really belongs to the patter songs, and it deserves to take precedence over most of them, but we may include it here as a representative of the songs which help on the story.   As a descriptive song, crowded with incident and humour in its every line, and with a happy moral at the end of it all, it holds a very high rank in the operas. In the humorous vein it is probably Gilbert's best and most typical lyric.

> Oh, philosophers may sing
> Of the troubles of a king,
> But of pleasures there are many and of worries there are none.
> And the culminating pleasure
> That we treasure beyond measure
> Is the gratifying feeling that our duty has been done."

Nanki-Poo's " A wandering minstrel I," with its varied moods and phrases, each change certainly emphasised by the music, is another fine narrative song. We have also Arac's " This helmet, I suppose "—and is there any more sublimely ridiculous scene than that of these dull warrior brothers divesting themselves of their armour before going into the fight?—and Richard Dauntless's breezy " I shipped, d'ye see, on a Revenue sloop." " The criminal cried " trio, which is also concerned directly with the action of the play, contrives a good deal of humour out of a grisly idea. Sir Roderic's " When the night wind howls " a song of ghostly revelries by night, is the cleverest essay in vivid descriptive poetry and in the creation of an eerie atmosphere. It is more graphic, for instance, than Dame Carruthers' fine song of the scaffold and thumb-screw of the grim old Tower of London, that sentinel " unliving and undying."

One other verse in this so-called narrative class must be mentioned here. It is one of the best that Gilbert wrote, and it shows him, so it has been said often, under the influence of Herrick.　This is Hilarion's

> " Whom thou hast chained must wear his chain,
> 　Thou canst not set him free,
> He wrestles with his bonds in vain
> 　Who lives by loving thee !
> If heart of stone for heart of fire
> 　Be all thou hast to give
> If dead to me my heart's desire
> 　Why should I wish to live ? "

We come now to a group which, for want of a better description, may be called the satirical and whimsical songs.　We have good examples of these in Lord Tolloller's " Spurn not the nobly born," Lord Mountararat's " When Britain really ruled the waves," and Private Willis's " When all night long a chap remains," all of them clever numbers, all of them affected by a whimsical modesty, and all of them to be found, of course, in " Iolanthe."　In the same class we may place " For everyone who feels inclined " and " Small titles and orders," two delightful duets in " The Gondoliers," and King Paramount's " First you're born and I'll be bound " in " Utopia."　Here, too, I think we must include Ko-Ko's enchanting " Tit-Willow," and certainly the Sergeant's " When a felon's not engaged on his employment."

" Take a pair of sparkling eyes " is in the forefront of all the purely imaginative songs.　It touches the idyllic heights, and how fragrant is its loveliness, how charming its picturesqueness !

One risks reproof by suggesting that possibly the music is not worthy of its rich inspiration. We have another lovely thing in Mad Margaret's " To a garden full of posies." [1] We have a lovelier thing still, judging it as light and picturesque poetry, in Yum-Yum's " The sun whose rays." It is the music and the stage picture—hardly the verse—that give charm to the Queen's " Oh, foolish fay."

For two fragments of really graceful fancy we should find it difficult to excel the " Princess Ida " trio :

" Expressive glances
Shall be our lances,
    And pops of Sillery,
    Our light artillery,
We'll storm their bowers,
With scented showers
Of fairest flowers,
    That we can buy !
        Oh, dainty triolet !
        Oh, fragrant violet !
        Oh, gentle heigho-let
        (Or little sigh.)

and this dainty favour by one of the Fairies in " Iolanthe " :

" We can ride on lovers' sighs,
Warm ourselves in lovers' eyes,
Bathe ourselves in lovers' tears,
Clothe ourselves in lovers' fears,
Arm ourselves with lovers' darts,
Hide ourselves in lovers' hearts."

[1] This was apparently an interpolated song. *Ruddigore* was produced in 1887, and the identical verses, presumably by Gilbert, had appeared three or four years previously in the *Sporting and Dramatic News*.

One song there is that so far has defied enumeration in any category. It is one of the supreme songs in Gilbert and Sullivan Opera. It is that joyous and invigorating pæan of praise to the English girl, sung by Mr. Goldbury, enviable man, towards the end of " Utopia." The last verse irresistibly demands quotation :

" Her soul is sweet as the ocean air,
  For prudery knows no haven there,
  To find mock-modesty please apply
  To the conscious blush and the downcast eye.
     Rich in the things contentment brings,
        In every pure enjoyment wealthy
     Blithe as a beautiful bird she sings
        For body and mind are hale and healthy.
     Her eyes they thrill with right goodwill—
        Her heart is light as a floating feather—
     As pure and bright as the mountain rill
        That leaps and laughs in the Highland heather.

  Go search the world and search the sea,
  Then come you home and sing with me,
  There's no such gold and no such pearl
  As a bright and beautiful English girl ! "

A great song truly ! Gilbert, whose mood is so often sardonic, wrote it in the later part of his career, and at an age when it becomes a habit to frown on the exuberances of youth. Here he is heartier, more confident, more human even, than he has ever been—a man with a zestful, robust faith in his own age, his own world, and his own people. Nowhere do we find him striking such a note of real jubilation.

Summing up, I suggest that we may choose the following as the six best songs in the operas, the selection being based in the main on the lyrics, and with the least reference possible to the musical accompaniments :

1. " None shall part us." (Strephon-Phyllis duet in " Iolanthe.")

2. " When I, good friends, was called to the Bar " (Judge's song in " Trial by Jury.")

3. " A wonderful joy our eyes to bless." (Mr. Goldbury's song in " Utopia.")

4. " Take a pair of sparkling eyes." (Marco's song in " The Gondoliers.")

5. " If you want a receipt for that popular mystery." (Colonel Calverley's song in " Patience.")

6. " Rising early in the morning." (Giuseppe's song in " The Gondoliers.")

I cannot expect that this list will have general approval. I may claim that it is a representative list, inasmuch as it includes only one from each group of representative songs, but there are many omissions, some of them grievous. Calm deliberation does not *always* succeed in disentangling an exceedingly difficult plot.

CHAPTER XXV

THE SIX BEST AIRS

In what manner are the six best tunes to be chosen ?
We cannot divide the tunes as we divided the lyrics.
Easily though we may distinguish the gay tune
from the sentimental one, the sparkling tune from
the reflective one, the boisterous tune from the
elegant one, they do not lend themselves generally
to definite grouping. We can make our pre-
liminary survey only by going from opera to opera.
And at the outset we are faced by what seems to be
an intolerable problem. It was hard enough to
narrow down the selection of the six best lyrics.
It is harder still to name six tunes from such a wealth
of tuneful material. I call them " tunes " here for
a very good purpose. It is the " good tune " as the
ordinary listener understands it, the tune obviously
pretty in melody and lilting in measure, that is to
be our one test of merit. It is usually a musical
tune, but it is not always a musicianly tune, inasmuch
as sometimes technical merit is lacking.

Sullivan was a writer of musical tunes, but that
is not meant to suggest that his music, regarding it
for what it is, is technically inadequate. Nor does

it suggest that his melody is "syruppy." Sentimentalism does seem to hover over a good deal of his operatic music, but it is not that cloying, stickily sentimental stuff in which he had wallowed as a ballad composer. At all events there are few traces of it after "The Pirates of Penzance." Gilbert's verse did not call for that mawkish music. It called for pure melody—a stream of pure melody that was also wholesome and healthy. And the great feature of this operatic music is that it fits itself to the words so perfectly. Sullivan had most unusual material to work upon, but he has persuaded us that he has given each song just the right melody and just the right rhythm, and that any more suitable melody or rhythm would be impossible.

If we may judge by the music alone, there is little doubt, in my own mind, about the best opera. "The Gondoliers" stands out by its sheer wealth of inspiration and its bountiful good spirits. Elsewhere, of course, there are airs that may excel any that it has to give us, and there are other operas in which the music, taken as a whole, is lighter and more charming. But nowhere is Sullivan surer in his work or more wonderfully inspiriting. In "The Gondoliers" there is a verve and an overflowing geniality that no other opera possesses. It is here alone—and perhaps the point is not too far-fetched —that Sullivan seems to have any kind of relation to Wagner. It was after Wagner had written "Tristan and Isolde" and got the iron out of his soul that he could conceive the splendid strains of

" The Mastersingers." And it was after Sullivan had written " The Yeomen of the Guard," with the tinge of sadness there is about much of its music, that his muse burst into the joyous vigour of " The Gondoliers."

It will repay us to look at this music more closely. No other opera opens so brightly. " List and learn, ye dainty roses " for the women's voices has a sparkling melody, as rich and as colourful as the stage picture. It is a lavish, decorative tune with a touch of sentiment in it, and the effect of it is very refreshing. " For the merriest fellows are we " for the full chorus is a still more invigorating melody. It pulsates with life and buoyancy, a light-hearted and rollicking tune, stimulating to a degree. With the arrival of Marco and Giuseppe the music takes on more the note of elegance. The duet for the two gondoliers has a strumming tune that is as soothing as a lullaby. A playful theme and a familiar nursery air are used during the game of blind-man's-buff and the " capture " of Gianetta and Tessa. The scene closes with another rich and inspiriting melody.

The Act I finale epitomises even better the composer's style. There is a little of everything except the madrigal element to which he is usually partial. Gianetta's " Kind sir, you cannot have the heart " is deliciously Sullivanesque. Don Alhambra's lines are in the form of the traditional recitative. This gives place to the crisp measures of the " Regular Royal Queen " quartet, and this in turn to one of the happiest and most lilting of all Sullivan's numbers, the Marco-Giuseppe duet, "They all shall equal be." And then the mood changes. We have the two young brides singing their wistful farewells—a tender and a very lovable thing. It should be noticed that its chief theme is reminiscent of that at the close of Act I of " The Mikado." It should be noticed also that the perfect cadence at the end is as near to hymn form as anything could be. Last of all comes the swinging chorus that brings down the curtain.

In the second act the music hardly maintains this flow of inspiration. Some of the tunes do not rise above the ordinary. But there are others which, while they are not conspicuously melodic, do show ingenuity in fitting themselves to difficult lyrics. There is, for instance, that clever setting to Giuseppe's " Rising early in the morning." " In contemplative fashion " reveals also an adroit handling of simultaneous themes and a crescendo of musical interest as the members of the quartet lose their tranquillity and work up to a quarrel. The Spanish cachucha, built in the main on only a handful of notes, has one of the most exhilarating of rhythms, and the sense of contrast comes a little later with the gavotte, a trim and gracious number that reflects like nothing else the rhythmical elegance of Gilbert and Sullivan Opera.

We must now go back to the beginning. The best two tunes in " Trial by Jury " are probably those of the Judge's hearty " When I, good friends, was called to the Bar " and the Defendant's smoothly flowing, " Oh gentlemen, listen, I pray." In " The Sorcerer " the musical inspiration is not very high. If a choice has to be made, it would be the Alexis ballad " For love alone," and possibly the ensemble to the quintet " I rejoice that it's decided." " H.M.S. Pinafore " is full of lively melody. Captain Corcoran's songs reveal Sullivan at his best in the earlier operas. Good tunes are also given to Josephine and Ralph Rackstraw, and there is that glorious outburst of bluff, happy-go-lucky patriotism, declining absolutely to express itself too fervently or yet too sober-sidedly, " For he is an Englishman." This air reflects a national characteristic extraordinarily happily. The words themselves are also as plain and matter-of-fact, as wholly wanting in argument or in emotion, as the National Anthem. " The Pirates of Penzance " is a mixture of hymn tunes and musical comedy tunes, many of them very attractive, though there is a suggestion that the composer is still feeling his way. Nevertheless, there is a clever use of contrasted themes in the Frederic-Mabel duet, and a still cleverer use of them in the great double chorus, " When the foeman bares his steel." Mabel's " Poor Wandering One " is a charming air—probably the best of those in waltz time—and there is the novel accompaniment to Major-General Stanley's " Sighing softly to the river."

Up to " The Pirates of Penzance " the music has been distinguished mainly by its purple patches.

From this point the melodic seam is much richer. The good tunes, while not necessarily better than the best we have heard already, are much more numerous, and we must tighten up the standard of judgment. In " Patience," for instance, there are more fine melodies than there have been in all the preceding operas. There is, for instance, the haunting semi-ecclesiastical air of the twenty love-sick maidens, with which the opera opens. There is the robust melody of Colonel Calverley's song of the Heavy Dragoon. Strictly, of course, it is not a beautiful air, but it has about it a good deal of robust military swagger, and it catches the strong rhythmic flow of the lyric. Similar to it is the incisive martial beat of the Colonel's " When I first put this uniform on." The Grosvenor-Patience duet " Prithee, pretty maiden," has a neat and an inviting melody. But the gem of the first act, in my own view, is the air to the Duke's " Your maiden hearts, ah, do not steel." Simple as it is, and witty as a musical illustration, it is really an exquisite thing.

In the next act we have at least two exceptional melodies, one the mellifluent air that redeems and adorns Lady Jane's " Silvered is the raven hair," and the other the enchanting air to Grosvenor's " A magnet hung in a hardware shop." I personally hold that, if genuine tunefulness is still to be the one guiding factor, this is the brightest, the most captivating, and to some extent the most elegant tune in the whole of the operas. It is associated with a clever lyric—one of the parable songs—and it gains by a charming stage setting. Later we have the trio for the officer-aesthetics, an ingenious tune that suggests the stiff, staccato movements of a marionette or some other mechanical toy. And, as a contract, there follows the very refreshing melody of the quintet, " If Saphir I choose to marry." The Bunthorne-Grosvenor duet about the commonplace young man has a tune effective only in the sense that it is also deliberately commonplace.

" Iolanthe " also opens with an engaging melody. Its daintiness enforces the contrast later of the " brassiness " of the Peer's chorus, but until the first act finale is reached, the only outstanding air is Lord Tolloller's " Spurn not the nobly born." In the finale itself there is a succession of fine tunes, beginning with Phyllis's argument with the Peers, proceeding to the bold ensemble of " Let us stay, madam," and leading up to the invigorating rhythm of " Henceforth, Strephon, cast away." The Sentry's song which introduces the second act has an attractive theme, but it cannot be compared with that of Lord Mountararat's " When Britain really rules the waves," nor yet with that very beautiful air to the Queen's " Oh, foolish fay." The Fairy duet " In vain to us you plead " has one of those fascinating little airs that we find somewhere or other in each of the operas. The " In friendship's name " trio has a joyous tune. Iolanthe's " He loves ! If in the bygone years," on the other hand, has a tenderness unequalled in any of the other plays.

" Princess Ida " is a feast of good melody. What could be more exquisite than the air to the trio " Expressive glances " ? It is like the scent of flowers turned into sound. Or what could have more jostling humour than Cyril's " Would you know the kind of maid " ? Or what could be finer in their own ways than the airs of Hilarion's " Whom thou has chained " or the Princess's " I built upon a rock " ? Schubert might have inspired some phrases of the Melissa-Lady Blanche duet " Now wouldn't you like to rule ? " And Handel most certainly did inspire that capital imitation of the rhetoric oratorio style, the amusing trio for Gama's sons, " This helmet, I suppose." If this were typical Sullivan, which without question it is not, it would compel inclusion in the final group.

We come now to " The Mikado." Here the musical atmosphere is exceedingly bright. Nanki-Poo's " A wandering minstrel I " is a collection of tunes, an effective contrasting of sentimental, patriotic and nautical strains, and the song returns at last to the dreamy theme with which it had opened. Following Pish-Tush's " Our great Mikado, virtuous man," in itself a brisk tune, we have the mock ceremonial air of Ko-Ko's entrance " Behold the Lord High Executioner," a fine piece of musical humour, and the lively current of that little man's " As someday it may happen." " Comes a train of little ladies " is one of the most technically difficult of all the choruses, and there is clever three-part writing in the trio for Ko-Ko, Pooh-Bah, and Pish-Tush. Yum-Yum's " The sun whose rays " has a radiant melody. " Brightly dawns our wedding day " is written, of course, in the madrigal style. The Mikado's " object all sublime " song, with its boldness and its well-marked rhythm, has unquestionably an air worthy of a great lyric. " The criminal cried " trio has also some delicious harmony for the chorus.

So far I have not mentioned any of the airs in the Act I finale of " The Mikado." They make collectively a remarkable group, and it seems to me that, although we are trying to choose the best separate tunes, we are bound to include this finale as a whole in the final estimate. After all, if we may take any musical passage of equal length, there is no better music in Gilbert and Sullivan Opera. Katisha's entrance gives it an unexpected dramatic turn, and we have dramatic music and lyrical music, intense music and cheerfully playful music, woven together with extraordinary certainty. This finale contains some of Sullivan's finest orchestral writing, and it moves on with a sure, confident stride to that spacious climax, an unapproachable piece of music in its own form, though the words could not have given the composer, it seems to me, any great inspiration.

From " Ruddigore " I propose to take six melodies—and very fine melodies they are—for this preparatory survey. The first of them is the

" I know a youth " duet for Robin Oakapple and Rose Maybud. The air has a charm all its own. Like many of Sullivan's best tunes, it has a sentimental flavour about it, but the sentiment is never " sugary." The second is that hauntingly beautiful air to Mad Margaret's " To a garden full of posies." The third is the madrigal " When the buds are blossoming," a better example, and certainly more descriptive, than the madrigal in " The Mikado." The fourth is the graphic, superbly orchestrated air of Sir Roderic's " When the night wind howls," and with it may be linked the eerie effect of the ghostly chorus " Painted emblems of a race." The fifth, an example of droll humour in musical form, is the " blameless " air to the Despard-Margaret duet, " I once was a very abandoned person." And the sixth is the flower and the oak tree duet for Sir Roderic and Dame Hannah. It is a sweet, caressing little tune, and if it is omitted from the last list, it will be omitted reluctantly.

" The Yeomen of the Guard " music is coloured by a touch of gentle melancholy. Phoebe's " When a maiden loves " is wedded to a gracious melody. Colonel Fairfax's " Is life a boon ? " has a lovelier melody still, and among the tenor solos this great song, a vocal pearl of great price, is quite unsurpassed. There is a real charm in the " I have a song to sing O " duet of Jack Point and Elsie Maynard. It is a most ingenious setting of a difficult lyric. The " From morn to afternoon " chorus has the only downright, hearty air in this opera. Clearly it is there in order to provide the dramatic contrast when it is broken into by the tolling of the bell of St. Peter's "Strange Adventure" has one of the best airs modelled on, or rather inspired by, old English music, but a greater quartet still, musically considered, is "When a wooer goes a-wooing." This is Sullivan the melodist moved by an incident of genuine pathos. It is a sad, wistful tune which almost draws a tear from the hearer, so surely does it sound the plaintive depths. It is the one number to which an encore is never permitted. It would destroy the artistry and effect of this wonderful song.

We need now take a glimpse only at the music of "Utopia." It is not Sullivan's best music, but it contains a good deal of very typical melody, and it ends with one of the most rousing airs in the operas. "Let all your doubts," with the dance that follows it, has a tripping measure that illustrates very happily the absurd, youthful capers of the Wise Men, Scapio and Phantis. Sullivan, too, is his own inimitable self in the setting of that refreshing quartet, "It's understood, I think, all round." And he has one of his boldest themes for the first-act curtain. The Drawing-room music in the second act is delightfully written, and after the entrance of the courtiers we have the splendid unaccompanied chorus, "Eagle high in cloudland soaring." The King and the Lady Sophy, who had a choice air for their first act duet "Subjected to your heavenly gaze," have a choicer one still for

their second act duet and dance, the delightful
" Oh ! rapture unrestrained." And before long
we have reached the broad theme which acclaims
the simple Utopian's full-throated homage to
England :

" Oh, may we copy all her maxims wise,
    And imitate her virtues and her charities ;
And may we, by degrees, acclimatise
    Her Parliamentary peculiarities.
By doing so, we shall, in course of time,
    Regenerate completely our entire land ;
Great Britain is that monarchy sublime,
    To which some add (but others do not) Ireland.

        Such, at least, is the tale
        Which is borne on the gale,
           From the island which dwells in the sea.
        Let us hope for her sake,
        That she makes no mistake—
           That she's all she professes to be."

And now we reach the summing up. I confess
that I approach the task with some trepidation.
We must still call them " tunes," and we must still
choose the tunes which, because they are rich and
glowing melodies, usually associated with definite
rhythms, have a spontaneous appeal. There is
a wealth of these beautiful tunes. And we have to
narrow down the number to six. After " much
debate internal " I suggest that, while there are
serious omissions, just as there were when we were
selecting the lyrics, the six to which we must give
our preferences are :

THE SIX BEST AIRS

1. Act 1 finale of " The Mikado."
2. " The Magnet and the Churn," song in " Patience."
3. " List and learn," chorus opening " The Gondoliers."
4. " When a wooer goes a-wooing," quartet in " The Yeomen of the Guard."
5. " Expressive glances," trio in " Princess Ida."
6. " Dance a cachucha," chorus and dance in " The Gondoliers."

Two details we may note before leaving this subject. One is that, while Sullivan wrote scores of attractive tunes for these operas, and while his music follows one easily recognisable pattern, there are no two tunes that are really alike. It shows how copious was what we have previously called his magical spring of melody. The second detail is that my own list of the six best airs has unconsciously paid tribute to the allurements of a well-marked rhythm. The six tunes, melodic as they are to a degree, have also the fascinations of a lilting measure, not even excluding the one that is in a melancholy key.

CHAPTER XXVI

TOPSY-TURVYDOM

EARLIER in this book I quoted a very apt definition of the plots of these operas. It was that they represented the conflict between the well-balanced mind of the serious man and the exuberant spirit of his impish counterpart. It would be well, I think, if we now ran through the operas with this definition in view, because in no other way can the character and wealth of their humour be focussed so clearly. In the course of this review we shall see how conspicuously the imp appears in the picture. Seeing that he is an imp, all he does is fantastic, but as at the same time he is the other self of the ordinary and serious man, what he does is never unrecognisably removed from reality.

We begin with " Trial by Jury." Judges do not ordinarily take the court into their confidence, disparage themselves and their office, or philander with pretty plaintiffs. The Judge we meet here is, not the " serious man " at all, but merely the impish counterpart of a Judge. It is the imp that makes him say and do these things. It is the imp, again, that makes him take sides in the case from the beginning, and to ask, being as " susceptible " to

248

feminine charms as a certain judicial brother, whether the lady in the breach of promise suit " is not designed for capture." " We've but one word, my lord," answers the foreman of the equally susceptible jury, " and that is—rapture." The jury themselves are in the control of the imp. So is the Usher. It is not usual for a court usher to crave condolences for " a broken-hearted bride." So is Edwin and so is his jilted Angelina. What the imp really does is to take a phase from life and twist it into a fantastic absurdity. It is part of the merry game which in these operas we know as Topsy-Turvydom.

In " The Sorcerer " it is also the unexpected, as the serious man understands it, that happens. Grenadier Guardsmen are not usually revolutionary theorists, nor do they usually hold, we take it, that the classes and the masses should be linked in the bonds of a romantic equality. Alexis is such a zealot that he has carried out a missionary crusade in beershops and asylums. This must have been rather novel for a Guardsman. Such a whimsical idea, of course, only an imp could have inspired, and an imp determined that everything shall be done by opposites. It is not the imp, but the effect of a magic love-spell, that turns all the villagers later on into amorous couples. It is the imp, nevertheless, that pairs the squire with a comely widow who is loose in her use of aspirates, and that joins a dowager of the old school with a vulgar vendor of " penny curses." In real life this is " not done."

249

" H.M.S. Pinafore " is probably the imp's master-piece as revealed in these operas. Nearly every detail in it is a comical travesty. It is not usual on a British warship for a captain to fraternise with his crew, to exchange compliments with them, and to assure them affably that he never descends to im-polite language. It is not usual for common seamen to make open love to their captain's daughters. It is not usual for First Lords to visit the Fleet with a retinue of women relatives, to compose a glee for the crew, to dance a hornpipe on the cabin table, or to insist the captain must say " if you please." And it certainly is not usual for a seaman to hurl defiance at his captain by the proclamation, lustily supported by his shipmates, that he is an English-man. There is something more in these situations than the licence usually allowed to the stage. It is part of the impish comedy to turn things upside down and make the odd the ordinary.

Then there is " The Pirates of Penzance." The pirates are sentimentalists who, in particular, would never do harm to an orphan, and who have adopted piracy, not at all because it is paying, but because of its " comparative honesty." Already we are knee-deep in Topsy-Turvydom. The pirates are peers, and fairly young peers too, judging from the fact that all of them are " single gentlemen." We hear a major-general confessing that, although he is " plucky and adventury," his military knowledge has " only been brought down to the beginning of the century." We hear the pirates state quite politely that they have captured his daughters with the sole view of marriage. We see a band of policemen, almost as sentimental as the pirates, shrinking sensitively at the suggestion that they should be ready to "die in combat gory." And once again we get the impression that the mischievous imp loves to jolt our conventional aspect of things.

"Patience" is not strictly a flight into Topsy-Turvydom. It does not, as it were, turn anything upside down, but rather it inflates or exaggerates an absurdity into a super-absurdity. The imp is seen at work, not in relation to Bunthorne and Grosvenor, but in relation to the Rapturous Maidens and the Heavy Dragoons. The women are classic figures, and their love-pining has almost a classic severity, but there is nothing at all classic in their methods of husband-hunting. One of the most humorous incidents is that when, having learnt that Bunthorne is to marry Patience, and having his very definite assurance that there is no chance for any of them, they immediately link arms with their old sweethearts, the Dragoon Guards. The soldiers themselves are equally an impish inspiration. Guardsmen thwarted in love might do many things—except adorn themselves with velvets and lilies and mimic the affectations of a popinjay poet.

With "Iolanthe" we reach probably the most complete overthrow of reality. In the first place we have to suppose that the fairies are the controllers of our politics. We have also to suppose that a number of very haughty lords should lose their hearts to a simple shepherdess. We have to suppose that they would plead with her to " spurn not the nobly born," and that these pillars of the British nation, their suits having been rejected, should steal in on tip-toe in order to watch a trap that is to divide Strephon and Phyllis. We have to suppose that " love, nightmare-like " lies so heavily on a Lord Chancellor's chest that, for want of distraction, it " weaves itself into his midnight slumbers." We have also to suppose that Peers do their courting in Old Palace Yard, that they marry Fairies, and that together they fly off to Fairyland. For. once, however, the imp has gone too far, inasmuch as it has lost touch with the world and soared entirely into fantasy.

" Princess Ida," which in essentials is a burlesque, does not properly enter the realm of Topsy-Turvydom. Still less does " The Yeomen of the Guard." This work, the one more serious work of the series, has a plot which does not overstep the limits of possibility. Somehow we feel that Jack Point and Elsie Maynard, Colonel Fairfax and Wilfred Shadbolt, are " human " figures that belong to our own world, and that the tender theme of the story, though not the actual details of it, belongs no more to Elizabethan times than it might do to twentieth-century England. This can be said of no other opera. In no other opera is there so little of make-believe or so much of the elements of romance and pathos by which mankind is eternally swayed.

We are taken back once more to the land of illusion with " The Mikado." Here we have to believe that a Crown Prince should join a town band as the second trombone, and that because of a hopeless love for a girl of very ordinary social position, he should become, still disguised, a minstrel roaming the country. It should be remembered that Yum-Yum was Ko-Ko's ward when he was merely a cheap tailor in Titipu. We have also to believe that in the course of a month this tradesman was arrested, lodged in the county jail on a charge that involved the capital punishment, released entirely on his own recognizances, and exalted at one bound to the Lord High Executionership. Seemingly this was one of the new Mikado's ironical jokes, and it caused the great officers of State to resign in a body, though one of them, Pooh-Bah, was ready to take over the collected offices and stipends and become everything from Premier and Primate down to Groom of the Back-stairs. It should be noted that most of the officers of State were held to be subordinate to the Lord High Executioner.

There is not much impishness in " Ruddigore." There is a full measure of it, however, in " The Gondoliers." The well-balanced mind of the serious man convinces him that in no practicable state of society can all men be equal. The impish counterpart tries to show that he is mistaken, and it conjures a pleasing picture in which honest sons of toil are courtiers, in which Jack is as good as his master or better, and in which even Republican principles may be grafted quite feasibly on to those of the Monarchy. We have dealt with the opera from this aspect already, and we have seen that, while the merry sprite may deceive for a time, the end is invariably the re-establishment of the well-balanced mind and the triumph of a robust sanity. This occurs in all the operas apart from " Iolanthe."

Last of all—for a study of " The Grand Duke " in this connection is profitless—we have the topsy-turvydom of " Utopia." Once again the imp plays with the idea of drastic and ill-digested constitutional changes. In " The Gondoliers " the scheme had been to abolish all class distinctions. That was a failure. In " Utopia " the idea is that a primitive country should re-model its social and commercial customs on those existing in prosperous England. And such is the zestful pace of the reforming movement that there is a catastrophe. English methods, the best and the worst of them, do not thrive in an alien soil that was not ready for them, and the serious man knew that before he was inveigled by the dancing will-o'-th'-wisp.

From this summary we may gather that the basis of the humorous conceptions in these operas is that, while the situations retain some contact with life, they treat it from fantastic and contrary angles. Compared with ordinary mortals, the characters seem rather to stand on their heads, to do many things in the diametrically opposite way, and yet to create for themselves the illusion that their way is the right and only sensible way. This, indeed, was the great vein of fancy which Gilbert first exploited in the Bab Ballads, and we are now going to see that the Bab Ballads were the very cradle of Gilbert and Sullivan Opera. It was the ballads that created and the operas that sustained for our infinite delectation this pleasant little realm of Topsy-Turvydom.

CHAPTER XXVII

THE GENEALOGICAL TREE

CURATES had a fascination for Gilbert in his Bab Ballads. In these gay verses they appear again and again. They are not heroic figures as a rule, but the satire that flits about their devoted brows is light, inoffensive and gentle. In the circumstances it is curious that not one curate strays into the operas. The only cleric there is dear old Dr. Daly. He was a pale young curate once, but when we meet him he is a vicar, and when we are parting from him he is meditating retirement into the congenial gloom of a colonial bishopric. He is the sole wearer of the cloth and does it infinite credit.

Gilbert never concealed that he plagiarised the Bab Ballads. It is a Gilbertian idea that an author can plagiarise himself, but the fact remains that he did go back on his earlier ideas and utilise them in the operas, sometimes as inconsequential embellishments, and sometimes as the main planks in his platform. That is why it is remarkable that the curate is honoured with no place in his operatic plots. In one instance, as we shall see, he re-told the story of two Bab Ballad curates, but the curates had been transformed into poets when they reached the Savoy. It was done in the interests of taste. It was one thing to caricature a pallid curate in a fireside verse and quite another thing to portray the type on the stage.

I think it a pity that one Bab Ballad ecclesiastic never found an immortal niche in the operas. He is Peter, Bishop of Rum-ti-Foo, who came to London from his balmy South Sea isle to attend the Pan-Anglican Synod. For the edification and amusement of his dusky flock, this amiable man diligently studied dancing and acrobatic contortions, and his dignity revolted only when the bright idea was suggested that the sight of their bishop hopping ashore on one foot, the other ankle held high in his hand, would delight the hearts of the simple Rum-ti-Footites. Later, to " conciliate his see," he gravely dressed himself in cowries, fastened feathers in his hair, tripped the native dance, and married a dusky lady. We should have liked to meet him again. A certain Eastern ruler there was, we know, who loved to find sources of innocent merriment for his subjects' enjoyment, and it is a pleasant speculation whether he had not some relationship to this most accommodating of prelates.

My statement that Dr. Daly is the only cleric in the operas calls for some qualification. He is the only principal who is a cleric simply and solely. Our old friend Pooh-Bah, of course, is Archbishop of Titipu. I suppose that Don Alhambra, by virtue of his office, would also be an ecclesiastical dignitary. It may be a quibble, but how does it come about that the Grand Inquisitor of Spain, a vastly important person, can spare time to visit Venice over a relatively minor matter like the succession to the Baratarian throne? We must also not overlook that there is a bishop amongst the ghosts of Castle Ruddigore. He it is who raises a lawn sleeve in pious protest when the ghosts suggest that their descendant should carry off a lady. He is " never satisfied."

It is an interesting matter to trace what may be called the genealogy of the operas. It is only in the later works that we cannot find the germ of the plot in the author's earlier writings. " H.M.S. Pinafore " has a veritable cluster of ancestors. Six Bab Ballads were recalled to life for it in a greater or lesser degree. In particular there is that idea of the changelings. It is met with for the first time in " The Baby's Vengeance." Gilbert introduced it in a new form in " H.M.S. Pinafore," and the mix-up of identities of children in their infancy is the pivot, as we know, of the merry absurdities in " The Gondoliers." Even the " Yeomen of the Guard " lays the ballads under a slight contribution.

" Trial by Jury " was not written originally as a stage play. Seven years earlier Gilbert wrote a burlesque of a breach of promise case for the columns of *Fun*. It was in that paper that much of his earlier work appeared illustrated by his own pencil. When it was revised later for dramatic presentation, it was done in cantata form, with no dialogue. This

was because the German artist who was to figure
in it, though said to be an accomplished linguist,
disguised her accent better as a singer than as
a speaker.[1] Actually she never played in this
operetta. It is not surprising that Gilbert, for a
brief time a practising barrister, utilised his knowledge of legal procedure, however irreverently, in
preparing this early operatic venture with Sullivan.
He had a trial run along the same route in " Trying
a Dramatist." In this piece, which is undated,
he had a playwright put into the dock to answer
a charge of writing a bad play. The Judge in this
case is a colourless creature. Witness follows witness into the box to testify that it was a " rotten
play." It probably was—but on reading it one
feels that its creator was throwing stones at glass-
houses. The whole affair is terribly dreary. But
one notices that the accused complains that the
cause of the failure was that the company had introduced unauthorised gags. Gilbert personally
was sensitive about that kind of liberty.

" The Sorcerer " is as adaptation of a story
Gilbert wrote for the *Graphic*. In the operatic
version he made sundry changes, but there remains
the magic love-philtre theme, and it turns a charming village topsy-turvy. In the story the mis-
chevious conspirator is a curate, and he places a
commission for a supply of the love potion with a
firm of magicians, whose offices are in the West
End in St. Martin's Lane. In the play the scheme

[1] Madame Parpera-Rose, who died in 1874, aged only 36.

is introduced, much more benevolently, by the Grenadier Guardsman Alexis, and this time the magician is John Wellington Wells, who has an address in the City. The magic love potion is a Gilbertian theme that was invented long before Gilbert. It is at least as old as Shakespeare. The dramatist admitted that this play was lacking in story.

For the forerunner of " H.M.S. Pinafore " one need look no further than the Bab Ballad about Captain Reece of the Mantelpiece. This was the worthy who

> " Did all that lay within him to
> Promote the comfort of his crew.
> If they were ever dull or sad
> Their captain danced to them like mad,
> Or told, to make the time pass by,
> Droll legends of his infancy."

Captain Reece was blessed with a horde of women relatives and gave them to his crew in marriage. In the opera the string of- " sisters, cousins and aunts," are transferred to Sir Joseph Porter, First Lord of the Admiralty. Captain Corcoran and Ralph Rackstraw are shown to have been changelings in infancy. The key to that idea, as we have noted already, is " The Baby's Vengeance." Little Buttercup has an unmistakable resemblance to the narrator of " The Bumboat Woman's Story." In this Bab Ballad we read of the cruise of the Hot Cross Bun. Its well-bred crew would surely have realised Sir Joseph Porter's ideal that " on the seas the expression 'if you please' a particularly gentlemanly tone implants." Actually, in this case, it would be a lady-like tone, for it transpires that these sailors were love-lorn girls in disguise, as ardent followers of their captain as the Rapturous Maidens are ardent followers of Bunthorne in "Patience." Captain Corcoran is clearly drawn from the hero in "Captain Reece." He has also some affinity with that military worthy who, hearing that he had been changed, at birth with a child who became a private, readily fell in on parade and allowed the ranker to be promoted into a general. You may read about him in "General John." Ralph Rackstraw, the able-seaman who sings dreamy love ballads and sighs for the hand of his captain's daughter, is a re-incarnation of the sad hero in "Joe Golightly." In aspiring, humble seaman as he is, for a love beyond his station, he is following in the footsteps of another nautical swain who figures in "Little Oliver." "H.M.S. Pinafore" is little less than a mosaic of resuscitated ideas.

"The Pirates of Penzance" may be traced only generally to the Bab Ballads, in which we find a number of funny policemen, but a more obvious derivation is that from an operetta Gilbert wrote entitled "Our Island Home." This play, which still exists only in manuscript, is curious in the fact that the names of the characters are those of the original players. They were Mr. German Reed, Mrs. German Reed, Mr. Arthur Cecil, and Miss Fanny Holland, while a fifth actor, German Reed junior, is disguised at the outset as Captain Bang. The idea is that the party have been marooned on a South Sea island after a world tour with Gilbert's "Ages Ago." Captain Bang, whom they meet, is a tender-hearted pirate who explains that in his early days he was meant to be a pilot, and that it was due to an alliterative error that he became a pirate instead. He is just completing his apprenticeship. From this we see that the Frederic of the opera, written nine years later, was just a "re-embodied-spirit." Gilbert, when in Italy with his parents at the age of two, was captured by brigands at Naples. It cost twenty-five pounds to ransom him—but the use to which he turned the experience made it worth every penny. "The Pirates of Penzance" incorporates one entire passage from "Thespis." This earlier work was in some of its details a theatrical satire. "The Pirates of Penzance," though it has no close resemblance to it, was also a satire on the transpontine drama, the old blood-and-thunder school of bold buccaneers and desperate daring.

It was in "Patience" that Gilbert intended to revive the mild Bab Ballad rivalries of the Rev. Hopley Porter and the Rev. Clayton Hooper. They were to be so irresistible with the ladies that in sheer exasperation the dashing cavalry officers transformed themselves into parsons. Something like this had happened in the " pale young curate " days of Dr. Daly. The ladies had forsaken " even military men " so that they might gaze on him

" rapt in adoration." Gilbert had completed two-thirds of the libretto before he decided on a wise variation, turned the curates into poets, and for some less obvious reason changed his Hussars into Dragoons. In doing this he was reverting to his original idea, an idea previously abandoned, so he tells us, because of the difficulty of dressing the chorus æsthetically. It is clear that, although the main outlines were undisturbed, he had to re-cast a good deal of the opera.

" Iolanthe " has its roots in the Bab Ballad that tells of a curate whose parents were a prosperous lawyer and a young-looking fairy. He was a ritualist who became a Mormon. In the opera the attorney has climbed to the summit of his profession, he is still in ignorance both of the existence of his wife and the fact that she was a fairy, the curate son is transformed into a shepherd, and he goes to Westminster instead of to Salt Lake City. In the Bab Ballads there is also a story of two noble lords who were thrilled by the charms of a periwinkle girl. This idea recurs, modified just a little nearer to possibility, when Lord Tolloller and Lord Mountararat lay their hearts and coronets at the feet of Phyllis. Strephon, a fairy down to the waist, and the rest of him mortal, reminds one of that Bab Ballad worthy, Captain Cleggs. This amiable man had a mermaid's tail, the result of going down into the sea to visit the mermaids, who chopped off his shapely legs. The Admiralty decided that he was only half a captain and put him on half-pay.   This they did on the not illogical ground that " a man must be completely legged who rules a British ship."

For " Princess Ida " Gilbert went back to his own " respectful perversion," as he had described it, of the beautiful poem of Tennyson.   In the operatic version, written fourteen years later, his model was obviously, not the original poem, but his own parody.[1]   It is still in the form of blank verse.   Lengthy sections of it are repeated textually, but songs and choruses are added, a few passages are expanded, and certain points are amplified. Gama's complaint that he " hadn't anything to grumble at," a plain statement in the earlier version, is used as the theme of one of the best songs in the opera.   Ida still has her long declamation, and the opera ends in the same way, an exposure of the apparent impracticability of her crusade for women's rights.   The three warrior sons are caricatured broadly to serve the purposes of comedy.   It is curious to find in " Princess Ida," a work of Gilbert's maturer period, lines like

> " For, adder like, his sting lay in his tongue,
> (his ' sting ' is present, though his ' stung ' is past.) "

and

> " *Are men*, she would have added, but *are men*
> stuck in her throat."

---

[1] The incidental music in this early operetta was adapted from pieces taken from popular comic operas of the period like *Ching Chow Hi* and *La Perichole*.

Was it due to an oversight that he failed to rid it of these vestiges of an obsolete style ? The pun was the fashion when burlesque had control of the stage. In the days when burlesque was his task-master Gilbert, one has no doubt, dutifully committed a number of puns, but they were a vexatious type of wit at the best, and he did not usually allow them into the operas. Apart from the instance under notice, the only outstanding example of the pun, and rather an unduly drawn-out one, is the deliberate play on the words " orphan " and " often " in " The Pirates of Penzance."

" Princess Ida " was very properly called a " perversion." Tennyson's poem is an epic. Gilbert does follow the main lines of the story, but he takes a great deal of licence with it, robs it of its nobility, and turns classic romance into very theatrical comedy. It was only in this form, perhaps, that it was of any service to him, but one has a feeling that he had an unsuitable subject. The Ida of the poem, hard and imperious as she may be in some of her aspects, is a more queenly and human figure than the one we meet in the play. Gama himself is debased. Thus is he pictured by Tennyson :

> " Cracked and small his voice,
> But bland the smile that like a wrinkling wind
> On glassy water drove his cheek in lines ;
> A little dry old man, without a star,
> Not like a king. . . ."

—a much more attractive and benign personality, whatever its defects, than Gilbert's meddlesome

misanthropist, a " twisted monster all awry." In
the poem Arac is a genial giant and the soul of
brotherly chivalry. In the play this man of thews
becomes, like his fellow knights, little more than a
dull-witted poltroon. In the poem there is the
noble description of the combat in which Arac, as
Ida's champion, overthrows unaided first Florian,
then Cyril, and then Hilarion (though that Prince
is not so named by Tennyson). In the play a
farcical stage fight ends quite the opposite way. In
the poem Ida's cause is upheld by the conflict of
arms, but the eternal woman rises supreme when
she succours her wounded lover, remembers his
bravery for her sake before he entered the lists, and
hears from him that

> " Woman is not undevelopt man,
> But diverse ; could we make her as the man
> Sweet love were slain ; his dearest bond is this,
> Not like to like, but like in difference.
> Yet in the long years liker must they grow ;
> The man be more of woman, she of man ;
> He gain in sweetness and in moral height,
> Nor lose the wrestling thews that throw the world ;
> She mental breadth, nor fail in childward care,
> Nor lose the childlike in the larger mind ;
> Till at the last she set herself to man,
> Like perfect music unto noble words."

There is beauty here where there is bathos in the
denouement of the " perversion."

" Ruddigore " traces a clear descent from " Ages
Ago." This was another German Reed play which

Gilbert wrote to music by Frederick Clay. " Ages Ago " is based on the supposed coming to life during the night hours of the pictures in an ancestral gallery. In " Ruddigore " this idea is used only as a subsidiary part of the play. In " Ages Ago " it is preceded and followed solely by a form of prologue and epilogue. The four ancestors, two of them men and two of them women, belong to four distinct generations, and all have been painted in the days of their splendour. One is a Leonardo da Vinci, another a Michelangelo, a third a Godfrey Kneller, and the most recent a Reynolds. They step down from their frames and make love with a delicious disregard of the distances of time or the closeness of any family relationship. It becomes a nice point who shall give consent to their marriages. The younger two look to the elder two because they are their seniors in age, whereas the elder couple look to the younger pair because, as the elders were hanging on the walls when they were alive, they are as paintings virtually their property. It is Gilbert nearly at his best outside the operas. Signs of the 'prentice hand are visible in the finale—the perplexing solution is cleared up in any sort of a way— but much of the dialogue is uncommonly good. The scene of the play is called Glen-Cockaleekie Castle, and Gilbert makes one of his characters speak in a broad Scottish dialect, though it does not seem to me that he is fully at home with the " language."

In " Ruddigore " we are concerned with the

family curse of the Murgatroyds. They have to commit one crime a day or perish. This is a wide variation on the legend that is exploited in " Ages Ago." The legend here is that each owner of the castle is doomed to die without leaving an heir, and the old place remains tenantless for a century, when the title deeds are discovered unexpectedly and the lucky finder enters into possession. Another century is, conveniently enough, just ending when the operetta begins. Nor is it an astonishing coincidence that the deeds are discovered before the end of the play. They are placed on the table by an ancestress before she returns to her frame, and they make the hero, with the usual luck of stage tenors, the new lord of Glen-Cockaleekie. The " ghostly " motive finds its way in a different form into " Ruddigore." Gilbert, too, may have taken a thin idea from a Bab Ballad, that entitled " The Modest Couple." This tells the story of a lad and a lass who were so shy and sensitive that they were married in different churches, and then went off separately on a honeymoon. This may have suggested the bashfulness of Robin Oakapple and Rose Maybud. Nothing in the operatic plot requires that these young people should suffer from shyness. The dramatist was merely using up some old scraps from his cupboard.

Gilbert, as we know, was making sport in the opera of the transpontine drama, the vivid stuff which thrived at places like the old Surrey. " Foiled —and by a Union Jack ! " hisses Robin Oakapple when Richard Dauntless unfurls a protecting flag over Rose Maybud. That, to be sure, was a bit of the real stuff, the stuff that could be counted upon to draw the delirious howls of the " gods." In the opera the use of this old Melville trick is like the creaking of some rusty machinery. What Gilbert did in " Ruddigore " he had done rather less cleverly in " The Sorcerer," in " H.M.S. Pinafore " and in " The Pirates of Penzance." And now and then there is a bitter flavour in his travesty. I fancy that he not merely disliked the transpontine drama, in which he would have shared the feelings of a good many people, but that he actually resented it, because it reaped a success which he could rarely harvest with his own non-musical plays.

In several of the later operas it is difficult to trace anything in the nature of a pedigree. " The Mikado " certainly owes nothing to any earlier poem or play. The Pooh-Bah who figures in the Bab Ballad is an African cannibal, and in no way may he be linked with his operatic namesake, whose burden of offices suggests rather that he is an aristocratic cousin of Mercury in " Thespis." A Japanese sword that hung in his drawing-room—he was a diligent collector of curios—gave Gilbert his first idea for " The Mikado." The sword is the one with which Ko-Ko still makes his entrance in the performance of the D'Oyly Carte Company. A similar passing inspiration, that of the picture of a Beefeater he saw when he was waiting twenty minutes on Uxbridge station, gave the dramatist the clue that led to the writing of " The Yeomen of the Guard."

This last-named work is reminiscent only so far as Shadbolt has a resemblance to the " gentle executioner " in the Bab Ballads " whose name was Gilbert Clay." " The Gondoliers " makes liberal use of the changeling motive which we have noted already in " H.M.S. Pinafore." Was the main scheme suggested also by the reading of the adventures of old Sancho Panza ? Certainly he, too, reached a country called Barataria in the course of his travels, and as soon as he reached it, " the bells rang out, all the people gave demonstrations of joy, delivered him the keys of the gates, and received him as perpetual governor." [1] Apart from these details the opera is original. The Venetians, it is well to remember, were in the old days always sturdy Republicans. " The Grand Duke " shows borrowings from both " Thespis " and " The Gondoliers."

In " Utopia " there is the only case in which the name of a leading operatic character is repeated. This is Sir Edward Corcoran, one of the Flowers of Progress, introduced to the Utopians as the representative of the British Navy. Whether this is the Captain Corcoran of earlier fame is an interesting problem. Seventeen years have passed since we saw him in command of the old " wooden walls " of

[1] This parallel is noted in S. J. Adair Fitz-Gerald's admirable *Story of the Savoy Opera.*

the *Pinafore*. There has been time enough for him to be transferred to a steam-driven warship and to gain his knighthood. But Captain Corcoran was shown to be a Rackstraw by birth, and a Ralph Rackstraw who became a Corcoran would be, we take it, Ralph Corcoran. Was Sir Edward the son of Ralph Corcoran, alias Rackstraw, and the lady we know as Josephine, and did he owe his amazingly rapid promotion to a little wire-pulling by Sir Joseph Porter, ex-First Lord of the Admiralty? Or was he that same Ralph Corcoran's brother? These are troublesome questions. Sir Edward Corcoran introduces snatches of the Captain's song from " Pinafore." But one notices then that he is a baritone. Captain Corcoran was a tenor. On the whole we are well advised to dismiss the theory that they are the same person.

CHAPTER XXVIII

FIRST PRINCIPLES FOR AMATEURS

GILBERT and Sullivan performances succeed or fail according to the measure in which they may have " atmosphere." It is an elusive thing to catch, but it wins through even when the acting, singing and chorus work are of an indifferent quality. It is not within the province of all amateur societies to command a strong caste of principals. It is within their power, however, to give a performance which, despite its technical shortcomings, has this refining factor of atmosphere. The invisible autocrat who contrives it is the producer. The audience do not meet him and they find his name only in microscopic type on the programmes. But he it is who is the real author of a successful performance. Gilbert and Sullivan owes much to the discrimination and taste of the professional coaches who act as the wise counsellors and guides in amateur operatics. They have it in their hands not merely to make or mar a given production but to give the operas generally a higher or lower estimation in the eyes of the public. Luckily, the cause has been ably served by these men, and their deserts are greater than we recognise.

272

Gilbert, as we have seen already, drilled his principals with the rigours of a sergeant-major. The present-day producer, who is dealing with the awkward squads, the amateurs, should be just as unbending. If he has not a will of his own, or if he is not allowed to enforce it, he should gracefully take his hat from its peg and depart. For Gilbert and Sullivan calls imperatively for discipline. It is a hard, severe school in which the rein of individuality, even in the case of the leaders, has to be held pretty tightly. Without discipline a performance, viewed as an artistic unity, all goes to pieces. It is different when amateur societies make choice of a musical comedy. Nobody minds, and the play does not suffer much, if the performers introduce their own jokes, their own gestures and impetuosities, their own exaggerated ideas of interpretation. As an amateur training-ground musical comedy is terribly happy-go-lucky.

Gilbert and Sullivan has set a new standard. It has brought the team spirit on to the stage. And when we begin to talk of the team spirit, we get near at last to the solution of an old, old question. " What," it is asked so often, " is the real secret of the appeal of the Gilbert and Sullivan operas ? " The invariable answer is that sparkling wit and enchanting melody are so choicely blended together. This is true only so far as it goes. A third secret of their success lies no less surely in their refinement and sense of repose. They soothe or refresh by their elfish lightness. In their influence on us they are never boisterous or jerky. The quality of refinement is obvious at all times, whereas the reposefulness of the operas affects us, as it were, subconsciously. We may be unaware of it if there is good team work on the part of the performers. We are very much aware of it, on the other hand, if there is restlessness and an attempt by individuals to give themselves prominence, in however subtle a fashion, at the expense of the play. We are aware of it because the element of smoothness has been destroyed. The illusion is broken.

The sense of repose may be simulated in various ways. Clearly it does not mean that the acting should be languid or spiritless. Gilbert's characters are not a set of marionettes. Even the women's rôles—and these are the weakest of them—must have a breath of personality. But the whole of them have to be regarded as figures in a satirical setting. And the best satire is always that which makes a pretence of gravity. It is in this spirit that most of these parts ought to be played. They should be serious. It may be an easy seriousness, the kind that is neither laboured nor forced, but there must be a touch of earnestness over the drollery. Some of Gilbert's men-folk do lead the laughter when they themselves have made a good joke. We must be indulgent towards that human trait in their make-up. In general the characters who unloose a satirical arrow keep a straight face and let the audience do all the laughing. Gilbert never under-rated the public's humorous faculty.

He knew the audience would see the humour of a situation without the actor's assistance.

A Gilbert and Sullivan play differs from most others because of its concentration of interest. The eye of the onlooker is focussed on one incident at a time and on one incident only. It has not to wander here, there and everywhere to note what this, that or the other performer is doing, and thus to get a jumble of impressions, few of them of any consequence. Gilbert will not allow the effect of a beautiful love scene to be disturbed by any concurrent situation on another part of the stage. Every detail of the *mise-en-scène* has to be centred in the incident that matters. If the chorus are there they must share in the interest. They need not " register " emotions in the downright way of the films, but if the hero makes a romantic avowal, they must show that they are genuinely surprised and delighted. It will never do to look vaguely matter-of-fact, just as if it is the re-telling of an old, old story. In no circumstances may the members show boredom or indifference towards anything that is happening. Nor must they stare about the theatre, look listless when a situation demands eagerness and expectancy, or suggest that they have any identity apart from the play. It may seem a small matter, but the young lady in the back row who is titivating her head-dress may distract attention, however momentarily, from the main situation, and thus set in motion an under-current of unrest that mars the stage picture.

Now, it may be objected that every dramatic production strives for the same concentration of interest, and the claim does not need to be argued. The difference is that it is a bedrock matter with Gilbert and Sullivan. Subordination and co-ordination, if one may put it that way, represent first principles in presenting these operas. Every member of the chorus must subdue the temptation towards mannerisms and gestures that would single him or her out from the rest of the company. They are mere tricks of vanity—often far too successful —to draw the audience's eye. And as deliberate acts of indiscipline they are blameworthy to a degree. One may illustrate all this by a reference to the Queen's beautiful song in "Iolanthe." During the singing of "Oh, foolish fay!" the fairies stand in line behind the principal with drooping heads and a motionless posture. The song gains immeasurably from such a perfect stage picture, one of the most artistic in the whole of the operas. It only needs one of the fairies to become a free lance—in other words, to defy tradition by staring about—and the charm of the situation has gone. Gilbert, who laid down the tradition, knew quite well what he was doing.

I am not suggesting, of course, that when the chorus are grouped around the stage they must stand rigidly, without stirring a muscle or flicking an eye-lid. There is a happy medium in all things. Above all else these operas want naturalness and they want spontaneity. What they do not want—

and it is a point that has to be laboured—is exaggeration. It may be exaggeration in the form of over-acting, or it may be exaggeration in the form of trivial embellishments which, if everybody considered themselves free to commit them, would soon disturb the balance and the spirit of the performance. Each of these works may be likened to a beautiful garden, and in that garden there are no sun-flowers, rearing a gawky and obtrusive head over the rest, but just so many clusters of those sweet and simple flowers that bloom in the spring. This may be a parable, but if you think it over, it conveys a great meaning. I commend it especially to amateurs who find it difficult to hold a too exuberant individuality in check when taking part in these operas.

The admonition is one which applies very definitely to the amateur who is playing a leading comedy part. Nobody would ever suggest that he should try to keep in the background. It is his business to be in the centre of things, and to give the hearty fellow his due, he invariably looks after this side of his job. But at the same time, if he is to be a success in these rôles, even the comedian must know the art of subordination, or rather he should know when it must be brought into play. If, for instance, the central incident of the moment is one in which he is not directly concerned, he must not be a kind of corner man in a pierrot troupe and be at pains to do " something funny." That conflicts with one of the sound canons of Gilbert and Sullivan. By this I mean that the audience's interest must never be divided between the central incident, which may possibly be a charming love scene, and some absurd and unauthorised bit of by-play. If he has been trained in the musical comedy school, where the comedian has usually full licence, the pitfalls are easy. A Gilbert and Sullivan comedian can often be far too funny to be good.

The comedian is really the mainspring of the performance. For better or for worse he stamps everything with his own quality. So long as humanity craves for amusement, so long will an audience pay its tribute of applause to the funny man, laugh at his every antic, and approve his most inartistic grimaces. And there lies the danger. The well-drilled actor can resist the intoxications of the footlights. He remembers that his part is only a part, and if it be a leading part, then leadership imposes obligations. The less disciplined actor goes all out for a big personal innings. Nearly all Gilbert's comedy characters can be made " funnier " than we usually see them, and it is a simple matter for a naturally humorous player to add points of his own, though this serves only to debase pleasant satire into farcical comedy. Only two characters are little the worse for over-acting. One of them is John Wellington Wells and the other is Bunthorne. And Bunthorne can be made an awful wreck when an unseasoned amateur plays him melodramatically.

Gilbert would never allow liberties to be taken by his professional players. He held that his humorous perceptions were at least as keen as theirs were and that he had as sure a sense of stagecraft. Seeing that the traditional lines of interpretation which he laid down have stood the test of time, and that they still show no obvious scope for improvement, one may conclude that he was right. Why, then, should the amateur think himself entitled to introduce personal touches which may draw a quick laugh, but which in some uncanny way make the opera less refined and reposeful? Under weak direction this is a common failing. The strong producer puts his foot down on it abruptly. But in doing so he is a more courageous man than you would suspect. The amateur comedian is a fine fellow, but he hates the control of the guiding strings, and successes in musical comedy sometimes give him that strain of " bumptious self-assertiveness " which, you will remember, affected one of the characters in " Ruddigore."

CHAPTER XXIX

THE ACTOR IN SHADOW LAND

It is the custom of the leading Gilbert characters to disclose their histories and their idiosyncrasies as soon as they appear on the stage. The reminiscences, as we have had occasion to note, are unusually frank, and they are presented with a very definite rhythm. They appear where they do and in the form they do for a good purpose. Gilbert is impressing the nature of his characters from the beginning. It is his invariable practice. And he intends that from the outset the nature of the character shall be impressed by the player, partly for the edification of the audience, but partly also for the good of the performer himself.

This is an interesting point in dramatic technique. It also supplies the basis of all good interpretative work in Gilbert and Sullivan Opera. The characterisation must be definite. Above all it must be definite when the player has just made his first entry. He must *feel* the part he is playing, he must feel in his bones the nature and the oddities of it, and he must feel it to the exclusion of everything else. Later, if need be, the strain may be relaxed, but this definiteness at the outset is vital.[1] The presentation of a part begins in the dressing-room. It is there that the player must lose his own identity and become, let us say, an exclusive and haughty person (by which we may mean Pooh-Bah), a diffident and pensive fellow (by which we may mean Robin Oakapple), or a romantic lover (by which we may mean Strephon or Nanki-Poo). In this way he will take up his stage cue already in the right atmosphere. It gives conviction to his work from the beginning.

And Gilbert, in this matter of making the right impression from the beginning, helps his principals enormously. In "Trial by Jury" the Judge reveals himself at once as a mountebank and a light-hearted cynic. There can be no doubt about the lines on which the part is to be played. In "The Sorcerer" John Wellington Wells has a good opening song by which to enforce his rôle as a glib-tongued magician. In "H.M.S. Pinafore" there are songs that give the key to the characters of Captain Corcoran and Sir John Porter. In "The Pirates of Penzance" a song impresses the erudite simplicity of Major-General Stanley. From the manner of Bunthorne's entrance in "Patience" the audience can have no doubt whatever that he is a vain-glorious egotist and a strutting hypocrite. In "Iolanthe" the Lord Chancellor has to be shown

[1] For this point and some of the illustrations that follow liberal recourse has been made to the practical hints given by Henry A. Lytton in his *Secrets of a Savoyard*.

at once as a kindly, sentimental soul who carries his dignity not uneasily, and there are songs and situations which give the impersonator all the scope he requires. "The Law," he insists, "is the true embodiment of everything that's excellent," and his manner must be in accord with his declaration that "I, my lords, embody the Law." In "Princess Ida" both Gama and the Princess have the material by which they may strike the right note on their first appearances. In "The Mikado" both Ko-Ko and the Mikado himself have songs which are the sounding notes for their performances. In "Ruddigore" there can be no doubt about the bashfulness of Robin Oakapple, the craziness of Mad Margaret, or the melancholy villainy of Sir Despard Murgatroyd.

Then we come to "The Yeomen of the Guard." Here there is the case of Jack Point and Elsie Maynard. They are footsore and weary, and they have been chased by the crowd, but they are anxious to please. The Merryman and his Maid are no ordinary strolling players. They can sing *and* dance too—a wonderful accomplishment. And Jack Point has a taste for pretty wit and nimble repartee. All this is made clear from their first entry. In "The Gondoliers," again, we are introduced to that "unaffected, undetected, well-connected nobleman, the Duke of Plaza Toro." Equally he is "very knowing, overflowing, and easy-going." There is sufficient guidance in these words as to the manner in which the part should be played.

King Paramount in " Utopia " sketches his own benevolent ineffectuality. And last of all in " The Grand Duke " there is Rudolph's frank avowal as soon as this miserly creature appears on the stage that :

" I never join in merriment, I don't see joke or jape any,
   I never tolerate familiarity in shape any,
      This, joined with an extravagant respect for tuppence
         ha'penny
      A keynote to my character sufficiently supplies "

—a pretty bad jingle, though it does, truly enough, proclaim the nature of the man. So do most of the entrance songs of the principal parts.

I have sketched these characters only in the roughest form, but possibly there has been sufficient to show that not only must the impersonations be convincing to begin with, but that the dramatist gives the fullest help to his exponents. It is true that these have been mainly principal parts, and mainly the comedy parts, and it is these which are, after all, the mainspring of a successful performance. But the rule applies equally to the subsidiary parts. There must be definiteness of characterisation. From the chorus ranks to the " stars " there must be complete absorption in the course of the story. This is a counsel of perfection in any type of stage production. It is, I insist again, a vital matter in Gilbert and Sullivan Opera.

What I have in mind at the moment is the amateur performance. In the professional companies the art of concentration is numbered among the first principles in the presentation of these plays. It is partly this art of stage concentration, deftly as it conceals itself, that makes them magnetic. Behind it is that scrupulous adherence to tradition and that insistence on conscientious and patient training. It is an asset which amateur bodies can rarely possess. The operas, nevertheless, have never been more popular with amateur societies, and the standard of production, based in the first place on judicious casting, is often remarkably high.

Gilbert and Sullivan has its own technique. It is a technique entirely different, for instance, from that of musical comedy, which does not call for the sinking of the actor's identity. The essence of it, as we have seen in the preceding chapter, is artistic discipline. It calls for team work, for co-ordination and subordination, and for an air of spontaneity which does not conflict with the sense of repose. The principal must have not only a good voice, but a thorough vocal technique, agile enough for the patter songs and sympathetic enough for the sentimental songs. He (or she) must have clearness of enunciation, no small measure of dramatic ability, a good presence and a good carriage. An interpreter of the leading parts must also have personality—or more properly magnetism, for personality is the possession of everyone in a greater or lesser degree. And, above all else, there must be an appreciation of satirical humour and its significance. It is the perception of and the gift of translating a form of humour to be found in these operas only.

In no circumstances is Gilbert and Sullivan to be " flung over the footlights." The lines cannot be shouted or the humour made blatant. Strident declamation is alien to this fanciful comedy, and in such an atmosphere the raucous voice is not merely false, but frankly vulgar. The key-note must be restraint. It must not, however, be dissociated from definiteness of characterisation, absolute clearness of diction, and naturalness of style. In all good Gilbert and Sullivan acting there is a touch of earnestness—an earnestness disguised by a natural easiness and pleasantry. It avoids exaggeration, alike in enunciation and gesture, but it avoids also vacillation or limpness. Excess in either direction is fatal to the spirit in which these plays have to be played.

The Gilbert and Sullivan world is the world of make-believe. To the lookers-on the stage is a little land of artificiality and inconsequence. But to those on the stage it is very much a land of reality. Life to them is real and life is earnest. It teems with surprises and novelties, with delightful adventures, and with engaging experiments. It is not they who see the incongruity of these things. It is not they who proclaim that they are the inhabitants of a land of happy pretence. Nor is it the business of the actor in this shadow land to do so. It is in an atmosphere of the credulous that these parts must be presented. Fantastic ideas may be regarded light-heartedly—for these characters, which have the simple faith of children, have the joyousness of children as well—but that these belong to the region of sane things is a verity that must never be questioned. The characters are the instruments of humorous satire, but they themselves are unconscious of it, though the audience sees it quite clearly.

From this it follows that these operas cannot be given with effect on any lines of broad comedy. It is too rough and unrefined a medium for such fanciful and elegant things. Loud and boisterous humour is bound to spoil the illusion and break the spell. If these operas are make-believe they can be presented only in the make-believe spirit. It is not an easy spirit to capture. Nor is Gilbert and Sullivan in its widest sense—whatever a few silly critics may say to the contrary—an easy field for the amateur player. It has its own methods—methods which the ordinary stage does not turn to account —and the public are more alert to inaccuracies and deficiencies than they can be in the case of lesser-known plays. It has been objected that the lines of interpretation have become too stereotyped. For my part I should say that, if this is so, they have been stereotyped on lines dictated by the wisdom of sound stagecraft and lengthy experience. Gilbert laid the foundations of the traditions, a succession of able professional artists have built upon them, and it has yet to be proved that they are susceptible to material improvement.

And what are these traditions ? I have tried to indicate some at least of them in discussing the art with which the leading parts should be played. There are also the traditions that every detail must have refinement, that every situation must have concentration of interest, and that every word, while it falls with a soothing cadence on the ears in the stalls, is deliberate and perfectly audible to ears at the back of the gallery. In these operas we must have neatness, we must have elegance, and we must have the sense of repose. For amateurs these are ideals that have to be striven for, and the culminating pleasure that amateurs may treasure beyond measure is the gratifying feeling that in these plays, which do give them something to strive for, they have attained as near to perfection as possible.

CHAPTER XXX

THE SAVOYARDS

In the course of this book I have touched little on
the historical or production side of the operas. I
feel, nevertheless, that if we are to give any reasonably complete outline of the factors that have made
them successful, we are bound to include some
reference to the artists who created the parts. In
an early chapter I likened the dramatist to the fabric
builder and the composer to the more feminine,
sensitive influence that furnished and adorned the
four walls, or verbal shell, that the architect shaped.
We may now extend the simile. It must cover the
family who tenanted that home, the artists who
lived in it, who animated it, and who made those
four walls ring with happy laughter and song.

We do well to speak of them as a family. They
were a large family, but they were very faithful to
the old home, and it was rare that they drifted away.
Many names appear continuously in the castes of
the productions. And these Gilbert and Sullivan
children worked as a team. The work was hard
and the standard exacting. I think we must agree
that there were no super-men amongst them, no

superlatively great figures in the world of the stage, and yet as a body they were ideally suited to comic opera conditions. Gilbert and Sullivan, if we must be candid about it, offers little scope for the super-man.

Let us take the case of George Grossmith. He was not a great actor and certainly not a great singer. But as a comedian he was inimitable. In his youth he was an entertainer, and an entertainer he remained, both on the stage and off it, to the end of his days. This supplies the key to his style. It accounts for some of his limitations, but it also accounts for his delightfully confidential way with his audiences, his effective use of quaint mannerisms and gestures, and his artless little tricks of speech. In his nimble wit in extricating himself from some odd stage predicament, and in his sublime gift of carrying off the ridiculous with an air of preposterous dignity, he had not an equal. And Grossmith's face, with its infinite expressiveness, would have been his fortune anyhow. It was as a born entertainer—the society clown, to use his own title—that he excelled in these operas. And doubtless what their chief comedian could do and could not do was always in the minds of the partners. They studied him as far as they possibly could. I wonder if you have noticed how " If you are anxious for to shine " might have been written for an entertainer who was to sing it as he sat down and strummed at his piano.

Grossmith's work, it has to be admitted, was a

little unequal. Sometimes, indeed, he was good where one would have expected him to be weak, and sometimes it was the opposite. He was not, for instance, the greatest Jack Point. George Thorne, an actor to his finger tips, realised much more completely the possibilities of that wonderful part. Grossmith was a fine Ko-Ko, a rôle that would seem to have been made for him, but his Ko-Ko was not, after all, as fine as Walter Passmore's. Two of Grossmith's best parts were Sir Joseph Porter and Robin Oakapple. It would be hard to find two more dissimilar characters, and his success in these rôles, one of them created on the eve of a serious illness, is a tribute to his versatility. And yet Grossmith's finest achievement was probably Bunthorne. It was a sheer revelation. Since his time Bunthorne may have been made more melodramatic, but the part he had to play called for acting power, often deliberate exaggeration, of which he had not seemed capable. In a sense he was assisted by his figure, by his little artifices of manner, and by his dilettantish ways. But it should be remembered that this was a part in which ordinary comedy methods, or the obviously funny methods, did not apply. Bunthorne is a humorous figure because he is unconscious of humour and because his egotism veils his own realisation of his absurdity. Grossmith's dry humour carried him through what, from his point of view especially, was a very difficult part.

Rutland Barrington had been an entertainer also.

He was not a great actor, he was not a great singer, but he had art, he had perfect stage diction, and he had a wonderful presence. Grossmith was charm personified. Barrington had charm as well, but there was more aloofness and reserve in his nature, more of the manner of the grand signior. And these attributes also served him well. There were naturalness and refinement in every part he played. But as Pooh-Bah he was supreme. It is a nice question whether Gilbert drew Jack Point with his mind on George Grossmith—more probably he drew him with his thoughts on himself—but I do submit that he drew Pooh-Bah with his mind on Rutland Barrington. The part fitted exactly so far as it represented the austere manner and the stately gait. It would not be suggested—it is clearly very far from the case—that Pooh-Bah's character was also Barrington's.

And here we reach an interesting point. Barrington has told us that he was greatly worried when preparing this part.[1] Gilbert was not satisfied with the lines he was taking. " It is no more my idea of Pooh-Bah," he told him, "than chalk is like cheese." Barrington, thus reproved, spent an anxious fortnight trying to do what was wanted, and in the end the two men arranged a quiet hour or two at the dramatist's house, where everything was put right. After the production Gilbert heartily congratulated the principal on an undoubtedly great performance   It may be surmise, but it is

[1] See *Rutland Barrington, By Himself.*

possible that Barrington's trouble had been that, contrary to his usual method, he had been laboriously "acting the part." It was not acting, but naturalness, that the part wanted. Barrington did well as the Judge, and he was the smooth, benevolent country vicar to the life as Dr. Daly.

If we must name the greatest of all Gilbert and Sullivan artists, the one with the most perfect all-round equipment, I think it must be Richard Temple. Here, indeed, we had an actor who was a great artist, a man who could give just the right touch of decisiveness and finish to every part he played. He was also a baritone of repute. Early in life he was trained in opera bouffe, and for a time he was on the grand opera stage, where I believe he once played Rigoletto. At the Savoy his versatility was exceptional. The man who played the aristocratic Sir Marmaduke also played the stunted and evilly Dick Deadeye. The man who made so Arcadian a figure of Strephon was the man who was so oily and saturnine as the Mikado. The man who was that superb old soldier, Sergeant Meryll, was also the sepulchral Sir Roderic Murgatroyd.

Temple, of course, had chances that were denied to some of his colleagues, but the fact remains that he had several small parts, and he did them all surpassingly well. I suppose his best rôle was the Mikado. It was an intense and vivid character study, full of sardonic cunning, and yet at times wonderfully benign. Whether he was the best of all the Mikados is a different matter—the rôle has had a succession of really able exponents—but without a doubt he was the pattern. Every good study of the Mikado we have seen has owed something to Temple.

Then we have to remember Courtice Pounds. He was a comparatively late-comer, but in the lyric tenor rôles he was, perhaps, unsurpassed. He had a fine voice, real intelligence and art in the use of it, and a charm and style of his own in his acting. As Colonel Fairfax and Marco, both of which parts he created, he had grateful opportunities. None of the other tenor rôles has such supremely fine songs, or songs which ask more, indeed, in technique and artistry.

In the woman's parts there were also several outstanding players. One thinks at once of Leonora Braham, sweetest of singers and most winsome of heroines, who created all the big soprano rôles from Patience to Rose Maybud. One thinks of Geraldine Ulmar, who came later and brought splendid talents and personal attractiveness, not least as the first of the Elsie Maynards. In Gilbert and Sullivan annals her name is one of the very elect. One thinks also of Jessie Bond, for many years the leading soubrette, the creator of many parts, a vivacious little lady who radiated happiness. One thinks, too, of Rosina Brandram, the owner of a glorious contralto voice, not always convincing dramatically, but a player nevertheless who was always improving. She was the first Katisha and a remarkably good one.

I have mentioned so far eight of the leading Savoyards. The list is far from complete. By right I should extend it to include notable figures like W. H. Workman, associated at various times, like George Thorne and Walter Passmore, with the Grossmith rôles ; George Power, the first Ralph Rackstraw and Frederic ; Durward Lely, who surprised us when he created Nanki-Poo and surprised us still more when he appeared as Richard Dauntless and danced the hornpipe surpassingly well ; W. H. Denny, that droll comedian and consummate character actor who first gave us Shadbolt and the Grand Inquisitor ; and Jessie Rose, in a later time one of the brightest and best of Tessas and Phœbe Merylls. And even then there are omissions. Coming to our own time, I speak only of one outstanding figure when I mention Henry A. Lytton, a worthy wearer indeed of the mantle of Grossmith.

If I have made selections at all, it has been to take them as outstanding representatives, no more and no less, of a great family. It was they who were, on the interpretative side, the makers of Gilbert and Sullivan Opera. They first took Gilbert's characters, invested them with warm flesh and blood, and gave reality to these elfs of his strangely whimsical fancy. They first took Sullivan's melodies and awakened them to our infinite refreshment and delight. They were the first bearers of the " tradition " of Gilbert and Sullivan. And, in thus giving form and comeliness to these characters, they also were great pioneers.

The Savoyards undoubtedly had advantages. It is not true, except possibly in one or two instances, that the parts were written round their personalities. But it is very probably true that they were written with some regard to their technical resources in singing and acting. Such an advantage is obviously denied to their successors. In any case they were directly coached by one of the very ablest producers ever known to the stage. Gilbert was a coach in a thousand—and a coach who could be and was an autocrat. They were also able to play these operas, not for a week at a time, and not in repertory form, but for months together. They introduced these works and set the standard. That has been their legacy. Exceptionally high though that standard may be, and hard of achievement for their successors, professional and amateur, little has been conceded with the passing of years. To-day, if anything, the standard is higher. It is noticeably higher in certain respects. But the foundation work was that of the Savoyards. They—one makes no apology for adapting the phrase—were the lighters of the new " sacred lamp." May it never be dimmed !

I wonder ! I wonder whether those words pay a greater tribute to pious hope or prophecy ! Will the light of these operas ever be dimmed ? Will their wit stale and their melodies lose their fragrance ? Is there in them, after all, something that is unsubstantial, something which does give charm to our day but will fail with a new generation ? For how long these operas will endure can be at best an idle speculation. The key to it is, not the likelihood of a re-action in the tastes of the public, though that itself is conceivable, but the fact that in due time their copyright protection expires. Until 1961, a date sufficiently far ahead for most of us, they are vested in the legatees of their original proprietors, and we may take it that while they remain in these hands the traditional lines of interpretation will be insisted upon. After that they will become common property. They will then be at the mercy of any showman who cares to take them and mangle and vulgarise them beyond recognition.

If the old copyright laws had remained unaltered half of the operas would have become liable to this violation already. The Copyright Act of 1911, however, now continues the protection of literary effort for fifty years after an author's death, and it is a statute for which we ought to be grateful. But for this Gilbert and Sullivan would have been in peril of being dragged into the gutter by the cheap and nasty exploiter. In his time the dramatist had many tilts at Parliament. And Parliament, in thus safeguarding the interests of authors for a longer period after their deaths, requited its tormentor handsomely.

It may be said that in America, where the exploiter has long had a chance to do his best or his worst, the operas have retained their popularity. They have been modernised, their action has been speeded up, they have been acted on new lines, and they have been given most spectacular settings. But what happens in America, where they are accustomed to these things, could not happen in England. Here there is the tradition, and the departure from it would be not merely violent but shattering. In New York a comedian, an Englishman, quite recently had to turn Ko-Ko into a gymnastic, spring-heeled Jack. He did " cart-wheels," somersaults and sundry other acrobatics, all of them apparently immensely diverting. Irreverencies of this kind show a deplorable lack of appreciation of the underlying spirit of these plays.

At the outset I suggested that Gilbert and Sullivan was a British art-form worthy of honour and well worth preserving. If that was my prologue so must it be my epilogue. I personally do not share the indiscriminating frenzy of those who have made these operas a form of fetish-worship. Nor do I share, on the other hand, the objections to them of the high-brow, about whose attitude there is often something so " deucedly condescending." It is the merit of these plays, again to apply the Duke of Plaza-Toro's words, that they are *not* " too unbending, too aggressively stiff and grand." If they had been, they might have represented a higher level of artistic endeavour, but they would have defeated their chief purpose, that of bringing into the monotonous rote of the common people the refreshment of wholesome laughter and enlivening song.

Gilbert and Sullivan is the heritage of the average man, the man who has no poses or predilections, the man whose simple craving it is just to be lifted out of the cares of the day. And these operas, unlike most other popular things, are not suspect of cheapness. They have real humour, they have unbounding melody, and they have charm and picturesqueness. The Englishman asks for no more and has often to be satisfied with less. Enough it is for him that their whimsies should lighten his road and that their melodies should echo sweetly down the vale of the anxious years :

> " Rich in the things contentment brings,
> In every pure enjoyment wealthy."

THE END

A LIST OF THE
GILBERT AND SULLIVAN OPERAS

	Produced
"TRIAL BY JURY"	Mar. 25, 1875
(Royalty Theatre.)	
"THE SORCERER"	Nov. 17, 1877
(Opera Comique.)	
"H.M.S. PINAFORE" or "THE LASS THAT LOVED A SAILOR" . .	May 25, 1878
(Opera Comique.)	
"THE PIRATES OF PENZANCE" or "THE SLAVE OF DUTY" . . .	Apr. 3, 1880
(Opera Comique.)	
"PATIENCE" or "BUNTHORNE'S BRIDE"	Apr. 23, 1881
(Opera Comique, and transferred to new Savoy Theatre, October 10, 1881.)	
"IOLANTHE" or "THE PEER AND THE PERI"	Nov. 25, 1882
(Savoy Theatre.)	
"PRINCESS IDA" or "CASTLE ADAMANT"	Jan. 5, 1884
(Savoy Theatre.)	

GILBERT AND SULLIVAN

Produced

"THE MIKADO" or "THE TOWN OF
    TITIPU" . . . . . Mar. 14, 1885
           (*Savoy Theatre.*)

"RUDDIGORE" or "THE WITCH'S
    CURSE" . . . . . Jan. 22, 1887
           (*Savoy Theatre.*)

"THE YEOMEN OF THE GUARD" or
    "THE MERRYMAN AND HIS MAID" Oct. 3, 1888
           (*Savoy Theatre.*)

"THE GONDOLIERS" or "THE KING OF
    BARATARIA" . . . . Dec. 7, 1889
           (*Savoy Theatre.*)

"UTOPIA LIMITED" or "THE FLOWERS
    OF PROGRESS" . . . . Oct. 7, 1893
           (*Savoy Theatre.*)

"THE GRAND DUKE" or "THE STATU-
    TORY DUEL" . . . . Mar. 7, 1896
           (*Savoy Theatre.*)